All in a
Day's Work

All in a Day's Work

Tim Bryan

Ian Allan PUBLISHING

For Jack and Katie, with love.

Front cover, top:
Traffic Department staff at Paddington.

Front cover, bottom left:
No 6000 *King George V* under construction at Swindon in 1927.

Front cover, bottom right:
Driver and fireman on the footplate of No 4079 *Pendennis Castle. STEAM/Kenneth Leach collection*

Back cover:
Signalman Blachall on duty in Reading West signalbox in March 1960. *STEAM/Russell collection*

Half-title page:
Pride in the job: Driver Prowse of Newton Abbot, seen there in 1947.

Title page:
The crowded interior of Newbury goods shed in the years before the Great War. Staff are using the crane to load the horse-drawn dray on the right of the picture. *National Railway Museum*

First published 2004

ISBN 0 7110 2964 4

© Tim Bryan 2004

Published by Ian Allan Publishing

an imprint of Ian Allan Publishing Ltd, Hersham, Surrey KT12 4RG.
Printed by Ian Allan Printing Ltd, Hersham, Surrey KT12 4RG.

Code: 0405/B1

Contents

Foreword

The inspiration for this book came from work the author did in planning the new displays for STEAM: Museum of the Great Western Railway, at Swindon, which opened to the public in 2000. A conscious effort was made when designing the new exhibition not only to show the wonderful exhibits which illustrate the history of the Great Western Railway but also to tell the story of the people who worked for that company and through whose labour and dedication the railway generally — and the workshops at Swindon specifically — became such an important part of our social and economic history.

Writing in 1980, the distinguished railway historian Professor Jack Simmons remarked that the history of Britain's railways had, up to that point, been written from just two points of view, either focusing on the growth of the companies themselves or concentrating heavily on the technology which drove them, in particular the development and operation of the steam locomotive, which has probably had more attention than any other aspect of railways. As he noted, there were (and still are) good reasons for this situation, since many of the historical records kept by the companies still survive, and in the postwar period enthusiasts and historians photographed and recorded details of steam locomotives before their eventual demise in the 1960s.

What has become apparent is that much less attention has been paid to the story of the people who played such an important part in the development of our railways. Most of the major figures like Brunel and Stephenson have been well chronicled in biographical surveys, but for the history of the rank-and-file staff the researcher has had to dig much deeper. In the 1960s a growth in interest in industrial archæology stimulated many to interview and record railway staff but also prompted the publication of an increasing number of books of reminiscences of staff who had spent most of their lives working for the railway.

A number of later books provide inspiration for those interested in railway life. Published in 1980, Frank McKenna's *The Railway Workers, 1840-1970* provides a national perspective on the role of railway staff, as does R. S. Joby's *The Railwaymen*, which appeared four years later, in 1984. For the Great Western Railway in particular, Janet Russell's *Great Western Company Servants*, published by Wild Swan in 1985, remains a definitive and evocative pictorial study of staff on the railway.

What is clear from a survey of this literature is that it is, for the most part, patchy. Some areas, like that of footplate staff, have been well covered, with the memories of drivers and firemen from most of the large Great Western sheds having been published. Other jobs, such as that of signalman, have also been well documented, with the evocative work of Adrian Vaughan doing much to promote the importance of this vocation to a wider audience. Some aspects of railway operation have, however, received little if any attention, and both the Refreshment Department and permanent-way staff have had little written about them. To find information about their working lives one is forced to look in other places, such as the *Great Western Railway Magazine* and reports and official documents issued by the Company itself.

This book draws on a variety of sources for its story. As well as using the written accounts covering the memories of staff no longer alive, I have dipped into some of the oral history testimony kept in the archives at the STEAM Museum, as well as talking and listening to ex-railway staff from all parts of the system, who have generously listened to my sometimes inane questions and told me their stories. I have supplemented their memories with material published and issued by the Company, so that rulebooks, reports and correspondence add further colour to the story.

What I have realised during the compilation of this book is that the information contained herein is only the tip of the iceberg; there are many more stories to be told, and many areas of railway life still to be researched. The book concentrates largely on what went on during the working lives of the men and women who worked for the Great Western and (after Nationalisation) British Railways

Western Region and for reasons of space does not really stray into the diesel era. Moreover, it mentions only in passing the important social activities generated by railway staff and their families — the educational, social and sporting groups in which railway staff participated — which were part of their way of life.

I am acutely aware that the stories told in the book are not definitive; talking to railway staff and reading their recollections, it soon becomes apparent that people's memories of what they did are all different! This book aims to highlight some of the activities and working practices but can never tell the complete story. In the book I have tried to show the highs and lows, the good and bad of railway life. For me, though, what shines through all the stories recounted is that, although working conditions may have been grim and times hard for many railway staff, they not only retain an affection and loyalty to the Company but, more importantly, remember the comradeship and good humour of working with others in the same situation. More than once in the course of my writing, ex-staff have told me that, despite all the difficulties, working for the railway was 'the best job they ever had', reinforcing my belief that working for the railway was far more than a job — it was truly a way of life.

Tim Bryan
Swindon
December 2003

Acknowledgements

No author can complete a book without the help of friends, family and colleagues who either directly or indirectly assist in the process. I am therefore grateful to the following, who have assisted by supplying information, photographs or advice during the writing of the book: Ted Abear, Alan Cheeseman, Mrs F. Cotterill, Tom Conduit, Ian Coulson, Brian Earl, Dave Ellis, Jack Fleetwood, Deborah Guest, Jack Hayward, Ian and Jane Hill, David Hyde, Rosa Matheson, Roy Nash, Alf Neate, Reg and Audrey Palk, John Plaister, Jim Sheppard, Gordon Shurmer, Stan Vickery and John Walter.

As well as those listed in the References section, who freely gave their time to answer my questions and talk about their life on the railway, I should like to thank the 'Meet the Railwaymen' volunteer group who talk to visitors every other Saturday at the STEAM Museum and have given both inspiration and information which has made the book immeasurably better. I am also happy to acknowledge the assistance of volunteers from the Friends of Swindon Railway Museum, particularly the 'Library gang' who have helped sort and catalogue the collections, especially the photograph library. Thanks are due also to the team that originally helped create the STEAM Museum. In the early days valuable work was done by Catherine Porter, who carried out many of the original interviews of ex-GWR staff. The help of Robert Dickinson, Sarah Finch-Crisp, Jill Jefferson Jones and project leader Julia Holberry was invaluable. I am also grateful to the whole team at the STEAM Museum — particularly Dee Curran, Felicity Ball, Helen Orford and Barbara Richardson — for their help and support during the completion of the book.

Finally, I should like to thank my wife Ann, not only for her support during the writing of the book but also for reading through the text and making many suggestions and corrections to my sometimes incomprehensible efforts!

Picture and text credits

The author is grateful for the permission of copyright-holders to reproduce pictures shown in this book. All images except those noted specifically in captions are reproduced from the collection of STEAM — Museum of the Great Western Railway at Swindon. Thanks are due to John Short, Director of Swindon Services, Swindon Borough Council, and Sue Stockwell, Head of Lifelong Learning, Swindon Borough Council, for permission to use this material. Every attempt has been made to contact all owners of copyright material reproduced in this book, but, where this has not been possible, apologies are offered in advance. Any omissions will naturally be corrected in future editions of the book.

I am grateful to Swindon Borough Council for permission to reproduce oral history interviews and other archive material from the STEAM Collection; thanks are also due to all those whose memories I have related in the course of the book, and without which the history of the railway would have been much the poorer.

Introduction

When one is describing the workings of the Great Western Railway, it is sometimes difficult to look at the Company without becoming somewhat overwhelmed by the sheer size and complexity of what by the 1930s had become a very large organisation. Certainly, by the standards of the railway industry today, the railway was huge. At its centenary in 1935 it was estimated to employ almost 100,000 staff, costing over £16 million per year in wages.

One has to consider also the sheer geographical size of the Great Western Railway, which by the 20th century had grown dramatically from the initial Bristol–London line proposed by Brunel in the 1830s. The acquisition of railways in the 19th century also brought the Company into the West Midlands, with large stations at Birmingham and Wolverhampton, and by the early part of the 20th century the system was virtually complete, with the creation of its two-hour route to Birmingham Snow Hill via the new 'Aynho cut-off' and a joint line with the Great Central. From the Company's headquarters at Paddington station in London the General Manager presided over an operation that stretched westwards as far as Penzance in Cornwall and to Fishguard in West Wales. As well as serving virtually the whole of the West Country, following the creation of the 'Big Four' in 1923 the Great Western gained control many of the independent Welsh railway companies, like the Taff Vale, the Neath & Brecon and the Cambrian Railways, which meant that the influence of the GWR reached far into North Wales.

The wide geographical spread of the Company was reflected in its organisation, which divided its operation into 12 broad operating Divisions, centred on London, Bristol, Birmingham, Chester, Gloucester, Worcester, Exeter, Plymouth, Cardiff, Newport, Swansea and Central Wales. Within each Division, the running of this huge operation was then sub-divided into various departments under the respective control of the Chief Mechanical Engineer, the Superintendent of the Line and the Chief Goods Manager, amongst others; the diagram on page 8 gives some idea of these.

The public face of the Great Western: a passenger guard waves a train off at Paddington in 1924. *National Railway Museum*

Men at Work: an unidentified locomotive crew and Inspector H. Flewellyn at Laira shed in a picture dating from the dawn of the 20th century.

Beneath the senior managers came various strata of officers, inspectors and local managers, who were above the staff doing the day-to-day jobs described within this book.

As we shall discover, the GWR operated for the most part under a fairly strict management regime; what might now be described as a 'Victorian' management style prevailed in many parts of the Company until World War 2. Speaking to the Great Western Lecture & Debating Society in 1905, Mr W. Dawson, a senior manager, argued that, although it was good practice to discuss working methods with staff, 'never discuss whether your absolute commands shall be obeyed', whilst discipline should be maintained if supervisory staff kept 'an iron hand in a velvet glove'.[1]

All staff were bound by the Company's Rules & Regulations, which by the 1933 edition had grown to a substantial 200-page document. They were expected to know these rules well and abide by them; in addition, a much larger and more comprehensive 'General Appendix to the Rule Book', which ran to another 300 pages, gave further detailed information on the operation of the railway,

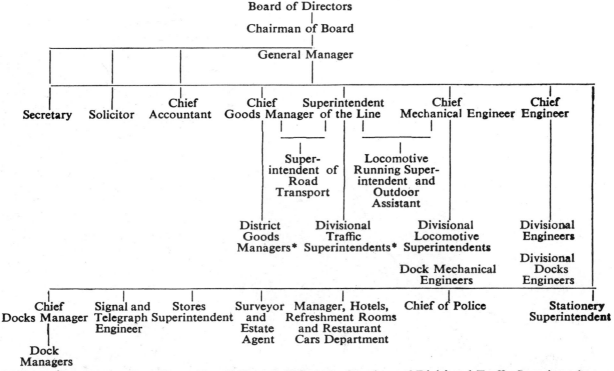

* NOTE.—In two areas (*i.e.*, Plymouth and Central Wales) the functions of Divisional Traffic Superintendent and District Goods Manager are combined under one officer designated as District Traffic Manager.

including as it did sections on signalling, loading of freight and station working. The Rules & Regulations referred not only to the safe running of the railway, which was, of course, critical, but also to the personal conduct of staff in their work and out-of-work activities. In places like Swindon Works, further additions were made, each worker there having an additional rule book giving instructions specific to that factory.

Staff paid weekly were reminded, on the application form they completed before joining the Company, that 'An employee must devote himself exclusively to the service of the Company, must reside at or near the place of his employment, attend for duty during such hours as may be required, be loyal and obedient and conform to all Rules and Regulations of the Company'. Some clerks signed a further declaration that warned them to 'observe the strictest secrecy with regard to all matters of a confidential nature which may come to my knowledge by reason of my employment in the service of the Great Western Railway'.[2]

The 1935 census of staff provides a fascinating insight into the internal structure of the Great Western, revealing

Above:
On the carpet: a posed picture, taken in 1924, portraying Great Western discipline before World War 2.
National Railway Museum

Below:
Staff at an unidentified goods depot on the most important day of the week — payday!

that, to control and administer the workforce, a total of 10,896 'Officers, Clerks & Supervisory Staff' were necessary — one of the largest individual groups of employees, excepting footplate and workshop staff. The Company divided staff into 'Grades', and the following table outlines the position in 1935:

GENERAL MANAGER'S DEPARTMENT
Officers, Clerks & Supervisory Staff	10,896

TRAFFIC DEPARTMENT
Station Masters	747
Passenger Guards	946
Goods Guards	2,450
Signalmen	4,356
Shunters	3,523
Ticket Collectors	435
Porters	4,088
Motor Parcel Van men	299
Horse Parcel Van men	103

GOODS DEPARTMENT
Goods Agents	81
Goods Shed Staff	5,384
Road Motor Drivers	1,369
Carters	1,143

CHIEF MECHANICAL ENGINEER'S DEPARTMENT
Drivers & Firemen	10,953
Locomotive Shed men	3,597
Carriage & Wagon Examiners & Greasers	819
Carriage Cleaners	1,163
Workshop Staff	13,762

CIVIL ENGINEER'S DEPARTMENT
Permanent Way Staff	8,896
Workshop Staff	2,949
Officers & crew of dredgers	145
Canal Staff	194

SIGNAL & TELEGRAPH DEPARTMENT
Linemen, assistants, wiremen & labourers	1,492
Workshop Staff	324

DOCKS & MARINE DEPARTMENT
Dock Staff	2,770
Officers & crew of steamers and tugboats	395

MISCELLANEOUS DEPARTMENTS
Stores Department	1,309
Hotels, Refreshment rooms and restaurant cars	1,514
Railway Police	320
Electricity Generating Staff	115
Charwomen and waiting-room attendants	524
Stationery & Ticket printing	91

The blanket term 'Workshop Staff' used by the Chief Mechanical Engineer's department embraced a multitude of trades and jobs done in the engineering industry. As we will discover in our survey of Swindon Works, within its walls a plethora of jobs, including those of boilersmith, blacksmith, fitter and turner, draughtsman, patternmaker, coachbuilder, were carried out. In this modern era some of these occupations now seem alien to us. Examples are the 'boshman', who tended the large tanks of acid (known as 'boshes') used to clean components stripped from engines, and the 'dings separator', a workman employed to separate, by a magnetic process, the ferrous and non-ferrous metal swarf and trimmings from the floor of the machine shops at Swindon.

Away from Swindon there were some surprising occupations revealing that, from their modest beginnings, railway companies had grown in the modern era to become multi-faceted organisations that did far more than just operate trains. The operations of the Marine Department, which included both docks and ferries, led to all manner of posts not usually associated with railways, including not only the crews of ships and tugs owned by the Great Western but also ancillary trades such as crane drivers and even divers, the job of the latter being described in the final chapter of this book.

The recruitment of staff into the Great Western Railway was controlled by a central office at Paddington, with a number of notable exceptions: technical staff, engine cleaners, workers at Swindon Works and what the Company classified as 'sea-going staff' were employed locally by Departmental officers. What the Company called 'new entrants' were theoretically recruited through advertisements posted at stations and offices, but in practice there were more than enough candidates who had already either written speculative letters to the railway or were the sons or daughters of staff already in the employment of the Company. A good example of such a letter (and which survives in the collection at the STEAM Museum) was written in 1924 by one George Drew, a Penzance fruiterer. In his letter to C. B. Collett, the Chief Mechanical Engineer at Swindon, he asks if there is any possibility that his 16-year-old son, also named George, can become an apprentice at the great works, as he is 'very desirous of becoming a locomotive engineer'. As well as noting that the boy had good examination results, he ends his letter with the plea that 'I may say I am a good customer of the G.W.R. for traffic in fruits and vegetables'. Unfortunately the Company's reply has not survived, so we shall never know if young George escaped from a life of fruit and vegetables in the West Country!

As we shall discover, working for the Great Western was a family affair, and many families, even today, can trace their

The Great Western employed a large number of marine staff. This picture shows Captain Thomas Pearn, who worked out of Neyland in West Wales.

railway service back through the generations. It is perhaps an over-generalisation to say that the Great Western was a 'closed shop' to those without family connections, but they certainly helped!

Before joining the Company most new entrants were required to pass a medical, and potential clerks had also to sit a stiff written examination which tested their English and mathematics. The Company noted in 1935: 'These examinations eliminate a number of the aspirants, a noteworthy feature being the large proportion of clerical candidates who fail in the educational test, and the number of girls who apply for posts as shorthand typists who possess a scanty [*sic*] knowledge of either shorthand or typing.'[3] It is probably true to say that, for many who wished to progress, the most difficult task was to get into the Company's service, for, once there, the ambitious railway worker wishing to progress up the ladder had (in most departments) the opportunity to do so, given hard work and some luck. Felix Pole, speaking in 1909 about clerical staff in particular,

highlighted the fact that when successful candidates were appointed they had little choice in the selection of the office or department in which they would work; this meant that they could be allocated to one of the more important departments like the General Manager's Office or a 'backwater', with little prospect of promotion.[4]

The Company, like many at the time, promoted and recruited from within. This meant that with a few exceptions — notably at Swindon, where the number of apprentices employed did not always equal the number retained at the end of their five-year apprenticeship — a job on the Great Western was a 'job for life', providing staff did not transgress to any great degree any of the multitude of rules and regulations already mentioned. Time and time again, staff reminiscences reveal a respect for the strict discipline imposed by Great Western management, tempered by a healthy disrespect for those who used their authority to either further their own ends or to bully and intimidate staff.

As in all walks of life, the quality and dedication of staff employed on the Great Western varied immensely. Many ex-firemen remember 'good' and 'bad' drivers who made their lives easy or difficult according to temperament or nature. One staff report from the 1940s clearly illustrates this point, as well as highlighting management attitudes and the language used by supervisory staff even in the dark years of the war. The report refers to a Cardiff Canton fitter (who shall remain nameless), injured just before the war; the fitter, it was noted, 'has shirked every job he has been asked to do and taken every possible advantage of his injury and would refuse to do even light work . . . if it did not suit him'. The worker, having asked to be moved to a clerical position, did not stand much chance of this, given his supervisor's comment that, if such a position were considered, 'it would not only encourage malingery [sic] but cause a great deal of dissatisfaction amongst the more honest and genuine members of staff'. The report concluded: 'It would be far better for everyone if his services were dispensed with altogether.' [5] The end result of this damning verdict is not recorded!

It was only the changes wrought by the massive upheaval of World War 1 that began to change attitudes and working practices. The pressures of war meant that the demands of the growing labour movement had finally to be recognised by the Company, changing the working landscape forever. However, whilst the labour troubles postwar, specifically the 1919 strike and, ultimately, the General Strike of 1926, did have an impact, particularly in the unionisation of the workforce, it was not until World War 2 that there were more substantial changes of attitude amongst workers and management. The growth of union power is mentioned by many ex-staff interviewed, sometimes with mixed feelings; few regretted the softening of the Company's draconian management style, but the sometimes difficult issue of demarcation was not always to the liking of some staff.

Reading the *Great Western Railway Magazine* and listening to the memories of staff that worked for the Company, one soon realises that most spent their entire working lives on the railway, retiring with many years' service. Taking a month from the magazine at random, one is struck by the length of service given by staff. In the March 1937 'Among the Staff'

GREAT WESTERN RAILWAY.

NOTICE.

Members of the staff who have absented themselves from duty without giving the notice prescribed by the terms of their service are warned that steps are now being taken to fill their places.

FELIX J. C. POLE,
General Manager.

PADDINGTON STATION,
May 10th, 1926.

[6]

It is not clear if this handbill was actually issued during the General Strike, but its tone is unambiguous.

feature, just a few examples of staff retiring are instructive. Mr W. J. Cook, Running Inspector in the Newton Abbot Division of the Chief Mechanical Engineer's Department, was recorded as leaving the Company's service after 47 years, whilst two colleagues, in the same Department but in locations as far removed as Chester and Machynlleth, each retired after devoting over 50 years to the service of the GWR and predecessors.

One particularly well-known individual example of progress through the ranks was that of Sir Felix Pole, the charismatic General Manager of the Great Western Railway from 1920 to 1929. He had begun his career as a telegraph clerk at Swindon station in 1891 and had worked his way through various positions at Paddington before eventually taking on the top job in the Company. Unusually for a senior manager working for the Great Western Railway (most of whom either retired after a long career or died 'in harness'), he left the service of the Company in July 1929 to become Chairman of Associated Electrical Industries.

Not every member of staff wished to progress or, indeed, had the opportunity to do so; as we have already seen, some Departments and areas gave better opportunities for staff to develop than others. Another important factor limiting progress was the ability of staff to move to improve their prospects. For station staff, signalmen or drivers the only way to better oneself would be to accept a new position at another location on the railway, which (again, as already seen) covered a huge area. For those with families this might be problematic. Lists of vacancies were circulated around stations and depots, and each month the staff journal, the *Great Western Railway Magazine*, printed a large list of changes amongst the staff that illustrated just how much movement there was. The staff changes recorded in the January 1939 edition ran to almost two pages and seem to confirm that most staff tended to move only relatively short distances for promotion; in the Traffic Department, for example, K. W. Pollard, a porter signalman at Ashley Hill station in Bristol, moved to Pensford, in Somerset. In other Departments staff appear to have been rather more adventurous; in the same month J. H. Taylor, a clerk in the Engineering Department, moved from Oswestry, in Shropshire, to Gloucester. Although there were those prepared to move, even in the

One of the war memorials erected by staff at Swindon Works after the Great War, situated in 'A' Shop in the Carriage Works.

1930s the Great Western remained an intensely parochial organisation; the majority of staff tended to stay in much the same place for almost the whole of their careers.

In general the reminiscences and stories recounted here are 'bookended' by the cataclysmic consequences of two world wars. The Great War of 1914-18 effectively ended a period of growth and expansion that had been prompted by the final abandonment in 1892 of Brunel's broad gauge; those 20-odd years of development had left the GWR in the enviable position of being one of the most up-to-date and enterprising railway companies of the period. The ravages of World War 1 effectively undid much of the good work done in that 'golden age', in terms not only of the huge backlogs in maintenance and building which resulted from the

railway's having to carry out war work but also of the tragic losses of life experienced in all walks of life during the war.

Over 25,000 Great Western staff eventually volunteered for military service during the conflict, of whom 2,547 — around 10% — lost their lives on the killing fields of the Western Front and elsewhere. The *Great Western Railway Magazine*, which early in the war had proudly printed pictures of staff who had 'taken the Colours' and subsequently made the ultimate sacrifice, eventually dropped the idea following the losses suffered at the Battle of the Somme in 1916, perhaps fearing that morale was being sapped rather than boosted by the gloomy news from France.

For those not drafted into military service for the duration, life for railway staff was not easy. Ordinary passenger services were curtailed, but, as the war progressed, increasing numbers of troop and special trains were run, including the famous 'Jellicoe Specials' — coal trains run by the Great Western from Pontypool in South Wales to Grangemouth in Scotland to supply the fleet anchored at Scapa Flow. For those employed at the Company's works at Swindon, the steady routine of prewar days was rudely interrupted as munitions and War Department work took over. Shortages of materials and, more significantly, labour meant that by the end of hostilities the Great Western Railway and its staff were in a run-down state.

The loss of comrades and workmates hit Great Western staff hard. Many of the young men who had left the railway to serve their country had not returned to their friends and family or had come back maimed or mentally scarred and unfit to resume a normal life on the railway. As well as erecting a large War Memorial at Paddington, at all major stations the Company installed framed Rolls of Honour, some of which still survive today. More touching were the war memorials, funded by staff subscription, which appeared at sheds, offices and depots. At Swindon Works almost every workshop had its own sombre reminder of the sacrifices made by young men from the town, and each Armistice Day a special service was held to honour fallen comrades.

With the euphoria of the Armistice gone, the postwar outlook for the railway and its staff seemed good. Unfortunately subsequent years were full of uncertainty and division as numerous labour disputes took their toll on the Company and its staff. The General Strike of 1926 had also created divisions that were difficult to heal. Whilst most operational staff opted to strike, management and supervisory staff generally remained at work, attempting to run a skeleton service on the railway. Once the strike was over, every name in the staff records was marked with either an 'L' or a 'D', denoting whether the individual had been 'loyal' (by working during the dispute) or 'disloyal'. On the union side there were similar repercussions, with those who had stayed at work being ostracised by their colleagues for years afterwards.

G. W. R.   1626

ARMISTICE DAY ANNIVERSARY.

WEDNESDAY, NOVEMBER 11th, 1931.

———————

The 13th Anniversary of Armistice Day will be observed in these Works on WEDNESDAY next by the stoppage of all machinery and locomotion for two minutes.

The Works hooter will be blown as a signal to cease work at 11-0 a.m. and resume at 11-2 a.m.

C. B. COLLETT.

Chief Mechanical Engineer's Office,
SWINDON.
November 6th, 1931.

A handbill to mark Armistice Day at Swindon Works, 1931.

Within a few years of the strike the fragile nature of the railway industry was tested still further by the Wall Street Crash; the effects of the Great Depression were felt years after the events of 1929, and workers at Swindon Works endured many years of 'short time' and layoffs before the demands of another war once again gave them more work than they could cope with. When World War 2 broke out in 1939 the Chairman of the Great Western Railway, Viscount Churchill, told that year's Annual General Meeting that 'those of us who went through the four years of the last conflict have an unhappy feeling of waking up, after an interval of broken dreams, to find the war which began in 1914 still in progress'.[6]

Staff who had lost comrades in the Great War must have viewed the outbreak of war with both dread and apprehension, although (as we will discover in a later chapter) the 'total war' of the 1939-45 conflict would be very different, and the role of the railway and its staff significantly greater than during the Great War. And, whilst fewer staff were actually killed in action, the world to which their surviving comrades returned after the war was very different. While they had been away, women had taken over many jobs previously seen as the province of men, and prewar discipline and attitudes had been moderated under wartime conditions.

The wartime placing of the railways under Government control meant that nationalisation was only a matter of time, for the four main-line companies were still weak after the struggles of the war period. The end of the Great Western in 1948 was not greeted with universal enthusiasm, and staff regretted the loss of identity that absorption into British Railways entailed. Morale was low after the war years, and recruitment even more difficult — a far cry from the selective approach adopted by the railway in the prewar era. However, all agreed that (for a few years, at least) the spirit of the old Great Western survived, and it was only the creeping changes brought about by the modernisation of railways in the latter part of the 1950s that began to alter attitudes and working practices.

For some, such as locomotive shed staff, the end of the

Above:
An unused ASLEF membership certificate from the Swindon branch office.

Right:
The end of an era: Swindon shed staff on the footplate of 'Hymek' diesel-hydraulic No D7010. Brian Kervin, on the right, is a volunteer at the STEAM Museum in Swindon.

steam era meant that working conditions improved significantly; the dirt and filth generated by the workings of steam engines was replaced by seemingly cleaner and more efficient diesel traction. For others, however, the end of steam and the modernisation process meant not only changes in working practices but ultimately redundancy, as the labour-intensive working methods so much a part of the Great Western were swept away. Stations, goods yards and branch lines disappeared, staff were 'streamlined', and even the works at Swindon — once the town's largest employer — began to contract in size (a process that would continue until 1986, when it finally closed after 143 years).

For whatever reason, the monolith that was British Railways seldom engendered the kind of loyalty staff had felt towards the GWR, even though working conditions and discipline might have been harder under the old regime. Staff who were employed during the long decline from Great Western days have mixed feelings about the process, and space precludes any analysis of a time when many retired rather than see the railway they loved brought to its knees. Instead, this book concentrates on an era when steam still dominated the scene and conditions for staff were very different from those experienced by workers in the railway industry today.

1

The Goods Department

The first freight services on the Great Western Railway began as early as September 1839, but, given that the railway had been built partly as a way of linking the two ports of Bristol and London (and that considerable benefits from trade between these two places had been expected), the development of freight traffic was only gradual. Not surprisingly, as the GWR network expanded so too did its freight business, but it was not until the end of the 1860s that goods receipts began to become more respectable. In 1870, for example, approximately 10 million tons of freight had been moved by the Great Western Railway, resulting in an income of £2,218,998.[1] It was around this period also that income from goods started to exceed that of passenger traffic — a situation that was to

continue until Nationalisation in 1948. Improvements in rolling stock and operation, coupled with a decline in the use of coastal vessels for the movement of goods in the latter part of the 19th century, meant that by 1910 the tonnage moved by the Goods Department had increased further, to 53,441,404, and the income generated to £7,111,348.[2]

Some measure of the importance of the Goods Department was that the man at its head, the Chief Goods Manager, was second only to the General Manager himself, even having an advisory seat on the GWR board. The department was divided into two distinct sections, headed by the Assistant Goods Manager (Inside) and the Assistant Goods Manager (Outside). These rather obvious titles marked a very clear divide. The Indoor Assistant was

The entrance to Paddington goods shed just before World War 1. The large office complex can be seen on the right-hand side of the picture. *National Railway Museum*

Cardiff Newtown goods depot, looking west, in October 1954.
Stan Vickery collection

responsible for managing the clerical side of the operation, and the staff under his control carried out a variety of tasks which included the calculation of rates charged to traders and other users of the services, the administration of claims against the Company for damaged or lost goods and the calculation of revenues which were shared when goods were consigned from one railway to another; clerical staff also checked consignment notes, invoices and other documents and were responsible for collecting money from customers, and canvassing businesses for trade. The Outdoor Assistant managed the loading, unloading and transit of goods traffic at depots and sheds, as well as the collection and delivery of freight by road. Although shunters were employed by the Goods Department within yards, the actual running of freight services on the line was carried out by the Traffic Department itself. Instead of the clerks employed 'Indoors', 'Outdoor' staff included porters, checkers, loaders, draymen and drivers. At its height in the 1930s the Goods Department employed over 10,000 staff scattered amongst depots and sheds all over the system, and this chapter aims to give a flavour of some of the work done in the larger depots.

By far the greatest concentrations of staff were at large urban goods departments such as those at Paddington, Bristol, Birmingham and Cardiff. A GWR booklet published in 1920 remarked that 'It is a truism that no two Goods Stations are exactly alike.' The differences between depots could be due not only to their structure and design, it continued, but also to their staff, 'and in a large measure by their history and traditions'.[3] What did draw goods stations closer, however, were the fairly uniform methods by which depots of all sizes were operated, and in general the structures and tasks described were repeated all over the Great Western system.

By far the largest depot was that at Paddington, and until World War 2 its staff complement was maintained at well over 1,900, including over 300 clerical staff. An article in the Great Western (London) Lecture & Debating Society proceedings in 1908 described the scale of the operation and went into considerable detail regarding the running of this huge empire, which, as one of the goods stations for the ever-expanding metropolis, received, sorted, trans-shipped and delivered over a million tons of goods a year. In 1908 693 horses were in daily use, utilising a staggering total of 577 road vehicles. The depot covered an area of over 13 acres, and 24 gangs totalling 260 men were used to unload the trains, paid on a bonus system to ensure that perishable goods, in particular, were unloaded with the greatest speed. The administration and bureaucracy for such a large venture was considerable; it was calculated that the offices in the Goods Depot handled more than a million items of paperwork each year.

The description of Paddington — the largest facility under the control of the Goods Department — can be contrasted with the following description of the shed at Cardiff Newtown provided by Stan Vickery, who began his career there during World War 2. Stan still recalls his time in the Goods Shed with considerable affection, although he would be the first to admit that the comradeship they enjoyed was more than balanced by the poor working conditions and sheer hard graft needed to do the job.

Cardiff Newtown was a large shed with 15 'roads' or sidings, each capable of accommodating around 15 wagons. In the 1930s more than 500 staff were employed there, and the paybill was recorded as being over £95,000 annually during this period. Some idea of the scale of the operation at Cardiff can be gained from the fact that in 1933 some 7,139,483 tons of goods were handled, although even this tonnage had been much reduced by the dark years of the Depression, for in 1924 over 10 million tons of goods had been dealt with! The financial implication of such huge amounts was clearly important to the Company — in 1924 the tonnage moved equated to receipts of over £1 million.

The staff at Paddington goods depot, pictured in 1912.

Above:
No 12 road at Cardiff Newtown in
October 1954. Note the porter's sack truck
in the middle of the platform.
Stan Vickery collection

Left:
A huge pile of goods awaiting movement
on No 13 road at Newtown. No wonder
fragile goods were sometimes damaged
in transit! *Stan Vickery collection*

Right:
A view of Newtown recorded
during a night shift in 1953.
Stan Vickery collection

A wartime view showing the unloading of a perishable load, possibly broccoli or some other vegetable.

Staff refolding one of the wagon sheets used to protect goods in open wagons.
These were manufactured at the Sheet Works at Worcester.

The effects of the Wall Street Crash had reduced this amount to around £839,000 by 1933. With such a huge turnover, the shed was a 24-hours-a-day operation, and staff worked a three-shift system, each overlapping the next. The first was from 7am to 3pm, the second from 12 noon to 9pm, and the final, night shift ran from 10.30pm to 7am. Staff normally worked nights (also known as the 'late turn') once every three weeks. Not everyone could cope with night work, and there were always vacancies in the Goods Department! The 'Irish Gang' was the exception to this, working permanent nights — a job not for the faint-hearted.

Throughout each shift, staff were organised into gangs of three — usually a checker and two porters, although on the late turn a 'caller-off', checker and porter was the preferred combination. Staff were paid at the rate of 10d per ton and during a shift were expected to handle at least 15 tons, to ensure a bonus on pay day. Not surprisingly, staff knew the arrival times of certain loads, and their location in the shed, which did not usually vary from week to week, since wagons were berthed in the same place for each destination. This meant that they could choose which wagon to unload, avoiding the smelliest loads (fish) and the heaviest and most awkward (Sheffield nuts and bolts packed in back-breaking wicker baskets). Another load to be missed if possible was the Crosse & Blackwell from South Lambeth depot; this consisted of about 10 tons of small, heavy boxes which took a long time to sort, thus preventing staff from unloading a greater number of wagons (and thereby maximising their bonuses).

On the night shift in particular, wagons were shunted into the depot at certain times. At 3am, for example, Worcester broccoli and other vegetables arrived and needed to be unloaded immediately. Two hours later the operation was repeated for Bristol traffic — usually bananas and other fruit. The sheer variety of goods handled is staggering — some were more appetising than others. In our hygienic age it is amazing to think that, even in the 1950s, bacon was transported in open wagons, being wrapped in sacking which was both very heavy and slimy when unloaded. Butter, meat and sugar were regularly shuttled from Cardiff Docks to the depot. The butter was moved in 56lb boxes, whilst sugar boxes weighed in at a back-breaking 2cwt. Another load best avoided was 'basic slag' — a by-product of the Port Talbot steel works and used as fertiliser — which weighed about the same as a sack of cement. Oxygen cylinders from Whitchurch in Shropshire were also unpopular with porters; Stan Vickery remembers unloading and stacking this heavy and noisy load very early one morning, much to the annoyance of a local resident, who appeared in his pyjamas to complain about the noise!

Unlike today, when staff are equipped with fork-lift trucks and pallets to speed up loading and unloading, Great Western employees had few luxuries. At Cardiff a crane situated outside the shed was used to unload very heavy items, such as iron and steel, but until the Beeching era most unloading was still done by hand. The tool of choice in the goods shed was the hand (or sack) truck. Starting a shift, the first task was to find a good truck — staff had their own

Railway Police did their best to stem the flow of pilfered items and often hid to watch for staff tempted to steal. The Company kept exhaustive records of goods which had been 'stolen, lost or pilfered', and two surviving forms giving details of losses from Bristol and Porth stations in the 1930s illustrate something of the problems faced by the Great Western.[4] Not surprisingly, Porth, being a much smaller location on the South Wales main line, had fewer losses, but in the fortnight ending 1 April 1933 the station agent reported the loss of one case of biscuits, four bottles of Hennessy Whisky, 29 packets of beef cubes and five bags of potatoes! Four years later, in March 1937, the larger Bristol Goods station had lost a far wider selection of items which included two steel bars, over 800 cigarettes, 100 bars of soap, a small box of sugar and a case of wine in transit to London from vintner Harvey's of Bristol. The forms listed the senders of the goods, their originating station and their destination, as well as the value of the items. Given the scale of even this small sample, it was not surprising that the Railway Police were kept busy attempting to keep the Company's liabilities to a minimum!

supply of oil to ensure that the wheels ran smoothly. These basic trucks were wheeled around the platforms and could handle up to 15cwt. There was little in the way of protective clothing either, the Company supplying an apron but little else. There was one further important piece of equipment especially useful on the night shift — a candle. Lighting in the depot was poor, amounting to dim DC lights, and the candle, fixed to a stick, was essential to ensure that porters could read the labels on packages and loads. Staff were expected to provide their own candles; if they did not have one, the Co-op wagons were raided, since these seemed always to have candles as part of their load!

As on the rest of the railway, discipline in the depot was tough, Stan Vickery describing the Shed Superintendent as 'God'. With the huge variety of goods moving through the shed, theft was not uncommon, but the ever-present

Even the largest depots were not immune from theft and deception. A report in the *Great Western Railway Magazine* for November 1916 described a labour dispute at the Paddington goods depot which developed after three of the Company's delivery staff and a foreman were arrested and charged with stealing and receiving flour from a London flour company. Applying its Rules & Regulations to the letter, the Company dismissed the staff following their conviction at the Westminster Police Court. Although the article does not make it entirely clear what ensued, it seems that staff at the depot felt aggrieved that their colleagues had been sacked, even though the Company had agreed to reinstate them if their appeal were successful. What seems like a 'go-slow' or work-to-rule appears to have followed, causing serious congestion within the depot. The outcome of the appeal was not revealed, but the article concludes with

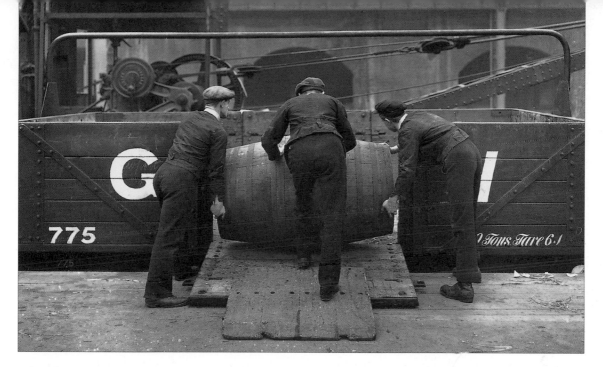

Loading beer barrels required care, to avoid damaging not only the barrel but also the toes of the goods staff!

a sly dig at the newly emerging trade unions then beginning to gain ground in the war period; there was, the writer noted, 'no excuse for any conduct of this kind now that the fullest facilities exist for the discussion of any real grievance on the part of railway employees'.[5]

Resourceful staff would often do their best to outwit the ever-vigilant Railway Police, and more than the odd sweet was 'liberated' from jars destined for sweet-shops on the GWR system. In Cardiff there were times when porters received 'free samples' of the local brew, if a barrel were 'accidentally' dropped! The label could easily be changed, and the barrel sent back 'empty' to its source.

Apart from unloading goods destined to be trans-shipped elsewhere on the Great Western network, staff worked to load the fleet of road delivery vehicles stationed at the depot. This operation was supervised by the Goods Checker, who had the task of ensuring that there was no discrepancy between the goods accepted for transit at the beginning of their journey and those delivered to the customer at the other end. Writing in the *Great Western Railway Magazine* in 1937, one such checker reckoned that 'there are few more interesting jobs on the railway than mine'.[6] Using a small, portable desk on the platform of the goods depot, the checker watched as goods were loaded onto road vehicles, ensuring that they were packed properly, given that they might comprise anything from delicate china to a piece of industrial equipment. A good knowledge of local geography helped ensure that material was stowed in the correct order according to the route of the van or dray. The checker also ensured that any chargeable ropes or packing were retrieved. The railway hired sacks to farmers and merchants, and even after Nationalisation a 1953 British Railways Western Region booklet noted that 'the vagaries of weather and fluctuations in yield of grain provide features adding to the problems of supply and demand', adding that 'sacks can be hired at reasonable rates for the rail conveyance of grain'.[7] The checker was also responsible for goods brought in for despatch by rail. As they were unloaded from the lorry, the checker made sure that the goods tallied with the consignment note and then directed the porter to the appropriate wagon.

Unloading goods from lorries or freight vehicles, as we have already noted, was hard work, and Company records reveal that it could sometimes be injurious to health. A copy of an accident statement completed on 13 April 1941 by P. J. Pearse, a 'lad' porter at Wiveliscombe station in Somerset, noted that 'Whilst assisting the carman to load whisky from a truck to the lorry, I sprained my back . . . after which I was unable to do anything'.[8] Whether the unfortunate porter was then allowed a medicinal 'tot' to revive his spirits was not recorded!

Further illustration of the amount of work done by porters is provided by another accident report, this time from unknown location. Mr A. C. Mouls, a motor-car man, reported that he had been loading laundry from a railway van on 18 August 1944. The weight of the load had been 3 tons, with bales varying from 1cwt to 3cwt. Apart from the assistance of van guard Mr E. Griffiths, he had had no help.

Mouls reported that 'the van guard mentioned that he was aching all over and I was done up myself'.[9] On a less serious note, a 21-year-old porter employed at Bristol Goods Shed was involved in an accident which, whilst not causing him any physical harm, could not have been very pleasant. On 24 July 1941 he was walking towards the Shed Superintendent's office when a member of the Engineering Department, working on the roof of the shed, dropped the contents of a tin of whitewash on him. In a letter reporting the incident the Assistant Chief Goods Manager noted that, although 3s 6d had been spent on having his suit dry-cleaned, the paint had not been removed and that 'the usefulness of the suit had been considerably reduced as a result of the accident'.[10]

The final task of the checker was to ensure that wagons were correctly labelled and sealed before they could leave the shed. The Great Western's 'General Appendix to the Rules' was most clear: 'Goods Foremen, Loaders, Shunters and Guards must take the utmost care to see that the contents of all wagons are evenly distributed, safely and properly loaded and secured where necessary'. Wagon labels, it added, should be 'in WRITING INK, not copying ink or pencil, which becomes indecipherable in wet weather'. In the Blackout conditions of World War 2 labelling — both of wagons and of goods themselves — became even more problematic. A Railway Executive handbill issued in September 1939 noted that, in order to 'facilitate the handling of traffic in the interests of both traders and Railway Companies, goods tendered for conveyance … must during the period of emergency lighting bear a white label clearly addressed in black ink or type'.[11]

Until well after World War 2 the Great Western Railway used horse power to deliver and collect goods from depots and stations. In 1930 the Company estimated that it had over 2,000 horses in its service, although by 1945 this total had dropped by almost 50%. Some insight into the job of the drivers who worked with horses can be gleaned from the Company's 'Cartage Instruction Book'. The 1939 edition noted that 'Teasing or playing with horses is forbidden as the practice tends to make them vicious'. Horses should be kept cool, it continued, 'and in as quiet a state as possible, otherwise they are likely to become overheated and get colic colds and other ailments'. As well as monitoring the health of their steeds, staff were expected to keep the iron and brass of harness bright and the leather 'clean and pliable'.

The railway used a wide variety of different wagons and trolleys, most built at Swindon, and each was maintained at the depot, usually by a fitter employed solely for the purpose.[12] The care lavished on the vehicles was mirrored by that spent on the horses themselves. At most depots the Company had purpose-built stables, and at Paddington the increase in goods business led to the original two storey-building constructed in 1884 being extended a number of times, so that by 1910 it had grown to an elaborate four-storey structure which also accommodated the staff needed to look after the horses, which numbered over 50. At Cardiff horses were housed in the nearby mint stables, built in 1912, and in 1945 Company records showed that over 110 were still in use, despite the introduction of motor vans and lorries. It was said that many of the horses knew their own way back to the stables at the end of the shift, as they did around the regular routes they trod each day! This was just as well in the case of some drivers, who either could not read and write too well or imbibed too much of the local brew during their lunch hour and were brought home by their faithful steeds.[13]

The motor fleet at Cardiff was maintained by a fitter from the Kite Street garage, located near the depot. This was just as well, since many 1930s-vintage lorries were still in use well after World War 2 and were not always reliable, particularly first thing in the morning. In the winter months, before the days of anti-freeze, a 'Frost Man' was employed who had laboriously to drain the radiator of each vehicle to prevent it from freezing. Many boys learned to drive in the goods yard, taking loads from the depot to the weighbridge, ready for the drivers; in the case of the horse-drawn wagons, there was a certain degree of amusement to be had, and more than one driver emerged from a tea break to discover that his horse was ready for the off, but in the wagon shafts the wrong way around!

An interesting insight into the life of a Great Western lorry driver was published in the Company magazine in 1938. London driver E. W. Clifton described his job as 'anything but humdrum'; operating what he called his 'iron horse', he spent the day not only driving but also as a 'canvasser, mechanic, furniture remover and clerk'. Unloading a heavy piece of machinery from his lorry, he described using a set of skids, a roller and the help of a 'small boy' to get the delivery inside the customer's premises. Other problems encountered included struggling to find change for a customer offering a pound note! Having returned to the depot for his dinner, he spent the afternoon delivering and unloading a container of 'enamelware' — pots, pans, kettles and the like. Since the container was railway property, the driver's responsibility was both to unload it and to check its contents — unlike today, when delivery drivers deliver but do not unpack their loads!

The driver's final duty was to go out on what he described as his 'evening collecting district'; goods for dispatch by rail were loaded onto the lorry for movement back to the depot. This, Clifton noted, was something of a puzzle; ensuring that a huge variety of objects, whether they be 'carpets, drugs, timber, pianos or paint', were correctly stowed was

The Company used mobile cranes extensively in yard work. This picture shows a Ransome & Rapier three-wheeled model. An example of these crude but effective vehicles is to be found in the STEAM museum at Swindon.

a difficult proposition, particularly in the wet. Additional to the obvious hazards which drivers could face in the course of a day through the lifting and shifting of heavy weights was the risk of injuries sustained from badly packed or loaded goods. A letter from the Great Western's goods depot at South Lambeth, written in April 1940 to Sharwood's (a company still manufacturing jam and preserves today) records that a carton of preserves being collected for delivery to Swansea caused a severe cut to a GWR loader, Mr W. C. Cotton, when one of the metal bands with which the carton was wrapped was found to be sticking out. Since hospital treatment was needed for the employee, the letter noted that it was 'formal notice of liability in the matter'.[14]

Although discipline, wages and working conditions were not the best, comradeship was a hallmark of the shed at Cardiff. Lack of opportunity meant that there were, as Stan Vickery says, 'clever people who shouldn't have been there'. The mix of people made it a fascinating place to work, and

the added ingredient of university students, drafted in to work during the summer months, led to interesting debates on religion and the like. Staff facilities were primitive — there was no hot water in the mess room and only fish-based soap to wash hands at the end of a shift!

Outside the shed was the goods yard; traffic unloaded in the open was usually material too large to be handled within the shed itself, requiring the yard crane or one of the mobile cranes which the Company increasingly employed from the 1930s onwards. Such goods included heavy items such as timber, stone, salt, lime and manure, as well as loads that were loaded and unloaded and moved by the consignees themselves. For staff, not surprisingly, conditions were much more difficult in the winter and in poor weather, when the already heavy and sometimes dangerous work became even more hazardous.

One of the most dangerous jobs in the goods yard was that of the shunter. Almost all railway staff interviewed about

The vast goods yard at Reading West in 1904. There is a wealth of detail visible for the railway modeller. *National Railway Museum*

their working lives will recount a story about some mishap or near-miss they witnessed during shunting, and it is probably true to say that shunting accidents accounted for more casualties than any other activity on the railway. Writing in 1939, Cyril Nicholls, an 'under-shunter' at Gloucester Old Yard, described his job as comprising two functions — sorting traffic arriving from other stations and marshalling trains for despatch. Trains arriving were split and then deposited in the depot's various sidings — a task necessarily completed as quickly as possible, especially if the wagons contained perishable goods that had to be unloaded and delivered rapidly.

Nicholls described shunting as being very much a team effort. In a large yard the shunting gang consisted of a foreman, a head shunter and two under-shunters. The head shunter controlled the movements of the shunting locomotive allocated to the yard, using either hand or lamp signals, and also supervised the under-shunters, who operated points and dealt with wagon couplings and brakes. The tool of the trade for the shunter was his shunter's pole — a robust pole approximately 8ft long, fitted with a metal hooked tip, used to lift couplings and to help operate brakes. Manufactured at Swindon Works, the poles were tested at the General Store on a machine that could check their breaking point, thereby ensuring that they did not snap on the job unless abused by staff! The misuse of shunter's poles was the cause of many accidents. In the Company's 'Safety Movement' booklet published in 1914 staff were warned that 'the practice of riding on a shunting pole is not uncommon. Everyone knows that it is forbidden. And why? Obviously because of its danger. Many an unfortunate fellow has attempted it to his peril.' The booklet also warned

Above:
When the retention of a steam locomotive was deemed to be too expensive, the Company used horse power to assist with shunting. This young shunter has under his arm the tool of his trade, the shunter's pole. *National Railway Museum*

Below:
The shunter's skill. Note the shunter's waistcoat, shiny from grease and dirt picked up during the course of his work. *National Railway Museum*

Left:
In this view the shunter is waiting for other wagons to be shunted up to his, so that, using his pole, he can hook the coupling over, ready for the next shunting movement.

Below:
A view of the work of the passenger shunter. The dangers of working in such close proximity to moving rail vehicles is very apparent, and it was no surprise that accident rates in goods yards and shunting operations were high.

In larger goods yards locomotives used shunting trucks, nicknamed 'chariots' by the staff, to assist in the operation. One such vehicle is coupled behind the '43xx' 2-6-0 at Weymouth in this 1947 picture.

that a shunter should not use the pole as a brake stick, thus causing it to snap; 'the chances are he gets entangled in the wheels', it continued. The shunter's job was, perhaps, more cerebral, however, anticipation and organisation being required to ensure that wagons were shunted in the correct order; the shunter's motto was: 'Never move a wagon twice when once would do'. Limited time and, often, limited space in crowded goods yards meant that training and intelligence were needed. According to Cyril Nicholls, 'Experience — and the instinct that comes from experience — are the important things. It is a rare job for keeping you on your toes — but I like it!'

At Cardiff another feature of the yard was the cattle pens situated up the line from the depot. As well as being responsible for the unloading and loading of livestock, staff were required to water cattle *en route* from Ireland to other locations on the railway. This involved unloading cattle from the wagons, and, even if 10 had been driven out, there never seemed to be enough room to get them all back in! A source of valuable overtime was the unpleasant job of hosing out wagons and cleaning the pens and track in the area next to the main line.

Stan Vickery recalls that staff in the shed had little contact with the clerks and other office staff. Colin Willott, born in 1928, began his railway career in the Goods Department

at Exeter in August 1944. Because he had an elementary School Certificate, he did not need to sit the clerical examination normally taken by railway staff; he remembered seeing the paper later and being quite glad of this, since it was so hard! Starting in the District Goods Manager's Office, he spent his mornings registering correspondence and filing. Afternoons were spent tracing claims for goods lost or damaged in transit — a task that must have been extremely tedious for a young man.

A fascinating insight into the way in which the Great Western Railway regarded its junior staff can be gleaned from an essay in a booklet published by the Company in 1920, entitled 'G.W.R. Goods Rates and Station Working'. Although full of information otherwise lost in the mists of time, some of its less formal moments are full of period detail. 'Young Railway Clerks,' wrote authors E. Ford and A. H. Warom, 'after the rough hewing of the first year or two's service, are still in a very malleable stage and very susceptible to correct influences.' It was imperative that they should not be allowed to 'muddle through', they continued, for, with 'intelligent coaching' and 'correct methods' there would be every reason to anticipate that they would become 'conscientious and efficient workmen'.

After National Service Colin Willott returned to work in the Accounts Office, where most of his time was spent

Right:
An unidentified
'Dean Goods'
locomotive shunting
in a small station
yard, with the goods
guard on the
verandah of his
'Toad' brake van.

Below:
The gloomy interior
of a 'Toad' brake van,
home for many hours
to the goods guard.

'adding columns of figures'; the job was done without so much as an adding machine — something he admitted he did not find easy. Moving to the Invoicing Office, he worked early and late turns, working $5\frac{1}{2}$ days a week. Eventually staff were given every third Saturday off, although they had to work late on a Monday to make up the time. Even in the early 1950s clerical staff still worked by gaslight; the gas pressure was very poor, and on a late turn copying detail from consignment notes onto invoices for up to seven hours was not an ideal situation. Originally staff worked on high inclined desks, but eventually management decreed that more modern facilities were necessary, so carpenters, presumably despatched from Swindon, were sent to cut the desks down to size. The lighting did not improve too much, however, and some nights it was hard to see in the gloom. Colin Willott also spent some time dealing with customer complaints and the management of railway containers, predecessors of the large goods containers we see today. Transferring to Reading in 1955 for promotion, he never returned to the South West, the perception amongst staff being that the nearer Paddington one worked, the better one's prospects were.

Returning to the description of the goods depot at Paddington, we find a very long and graphic account of the bureaucracy and paperwork necessary to run such a huge undertaking. In 1908 new office accommodation for clerical staff had recently been provided, replacing arrangements whereby staff had been housed in 'every hole and corner that could be utilised, amid conditions which that became unhealthy and unsanitary'.[15] At this time there were 364 staff employed at the Paddington shed alone, Another illustration might be the fact that the clerical staff were responsible for the production of up to 2,000 delivery sheets each day for

STATIONS	Arrival H.M.	Departure H.M.	Late away from Station H. M.	Overtime at Station H. M.	Lost by Engine M.	Shunting MINS 1	Station truck work MINS 2	Standing at Signals Train ahead MINS 3	Waiting for Trains to pass MINS 4	Other causes MINS 5	Loaded Goods	Coal and other Minerals	Cattle	Empties	Loaded Goods	Coal and other Minerals	Cattle	Empties	Loaded	Empty	Remarks as to Detention at Stations and in running.
Slough W6		8.18	18			10				8	1	22		3					23	3	Engine Lal from Windsor
Station	8.22	8.32	14			5	5					1		4					24	7	
Langley	8.40	9.33	3			20	5	28			1			2					25	9	9.5 P 9.25
Iver	check to Lost																				
W Drayton	9.47	10.13	18	11		15	3	5		3					10	1	5		19	19	Water
Hayes	10.23	10.53	8			30									5	2	2		19	22 2	
Southall	11.0																				
K Ealing	11.5	11.20		15				15													
Ealing B	11.25	1.40		2 15				135													old Oak unable take train
Acton W	1.45	7.10		5 25				325													
Friars J.	7.15	7.27		12				12													
6 Oak W	7.30	8.8		38				38													
6 Oak C	8.10														1	21	2				
Total											28		21		28		21				

LATE ARRIVAL

General Remarks, Occurrences to Train, Causes of Delay, and suggestions for improvement of working.

State of weather during Journey; if wet, frost, fog, or snow, between what points.
Eng to Acton Thick fog here

Working in _____ Division.

	Date.	Time.	From	To	Total time occupied including all stops in Division HOURS MINS.	Late at Destination HOURS MINS.	Number of wagons under maximum load at point of greatest load.
This Report must be ACCURATELY filled up, and sent to the Divisional Superintendent's Office immediately the journey is completed. Guards must fill in names of Stations; give particulars of all Wagons conveyed carrying over 10 tons in the "Remarks" column, and when sheeted for Trains in past give description and times of Trains which pass.	10/2/15	8.0 p.m	Slough W6	6 Oak Com	12 10	8 25	12

A Goods Train Record, compiled by the guard, from 1915.

horse-car men; these would then be checked at the end of a shift, and the car men be paid bonuses according to the amount they had shifted over and above the minimum. In 1908 a one-horse team needed to shift between 12 and 15 tons of goods per week before a bonus was paid, whereas the large four-horse team needed to shift over 60 tons. It was reported that between 80 and 90% of staff did achieve their targets, and as a result car men were paid 10d per ton and van guards 3d per ton.

Away from the larger goods depots the routine of delivering wagons to smaller station goods yards and of shunting and unloading was the responsibility of various members of staff. Once trains had been marshalled at larger goods depots and yards they were put under the control of the goods guard, who, somewhat confusingly, was employed

not by the Goods Department but by the Traffic Department. Having signed on duty and collected his 'standard kit', which included a set of red and green flags, emergency detonators and any special notices about the route over which he was to work, he was responsible for checking that all the wagons in his train were in good order and any loads securely roped or covered with protective tarpaulin sheeting. He also checked that all wagons were properly labelled on both sides with their destination.

Once the goods guard had conferred with both the locomotive crew and goods-yard staff, the train was ready to leave. Whilst the train was in motion he sat in his brake van, keeping a look-out for signals and, when passing signalboxes, any hand signals from signalmen. In the days before the adoption of continuously braked trains it was also

A 'Dean Goods' 0-6-0 on a local goods train in the 1930s. *National Railway Museum*

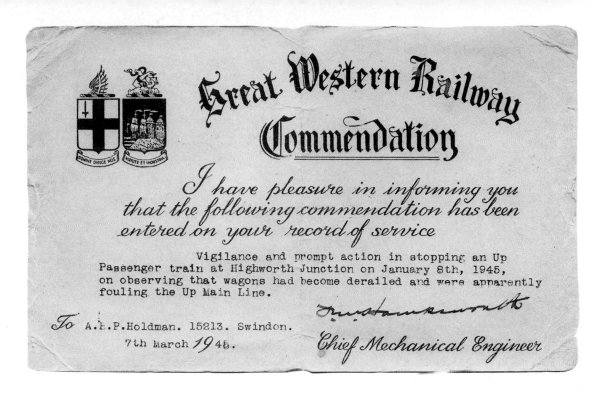

Great Western Railway
Commendation

I have pleasure in informing you that the following commendation has been entered on your record of service

Vigilance and prompt action in stopping an Up
Passenger train at Highworth Junction on January 8th, 1945,
on observing that wagons had become derailed and were apparently
fouling the Up Main Line.

To A.E.P.Holdman. 15213. Swindon.
7th March 1945.

Chief Mechanical Engineer

A GWR commendation awarded to an alert guard in the 1940s.

the guard's responsibility to assist the locomotive crew in slowing the train by the application of the hand brake in his van. Skill and experience were required, not only in judging where to apply the brake on a particular route but also in ensuring that any application of the brake did not result in the couplings of the train 'snatching', which could, in extreme circumstances, cause couplings to snap and a train to become divided — not a situation to be countenanced with any enthusiasm!

More laborious was the task facing the guard at the top of many heavy gradients. Goods trains not fitted with a vacuum brake were brought to a stand, whereupon the guard would have to walk down the ballast, pinning down enough of the hand brakes on individual wagons to allow the train to proceed down the incline under control; otherwise the combined power of the locomotive brakes and the brake van itself would be insufficient to prevent the train from running away. At the bottom of the gradient the guard would have to get out again and release all the brakes before the train could proceed. Given this long-winded process, it was no wonder that goods-train journeys could at times be lengthy!

Writing in the *Great Western Railway Magazine* in 1937, goods guard E. H. Smith, based at Severn Tunnel Junction, noted that his job called for 'plenty of common sense, as well as a thorough knowledge of the rules; constant vigilance is also necessary and, in emergencies, coolness and

judgement'.[16] Another facet of the job mentioned both by E. H. Smith and by other guards was the solitary nature of the role. It could be lonely sitting in a brake van for hours and hours, particularly at night, without anyone to talk to, whilst at the same time needing to remain alert and ready to respond to any emergency. Smith had spent over 25 years as a guard but concluded ruefully that 'loneliness is no disadvantage' and that whilst he was on duty his own company was preferable to anyone else's!

A welcome break from the loneliness and monotony of the guard's job came in delivering and collecting traffic at stations *en route*. Based at Oswestry, I. M. Evans described his job in 1938 as that of a 'humble goods guard' whose train 'stops at just those tiny village stations through which the other fellow just passes with disdain'.[17] His now evocative description of his local goods train, consisting of wagons loaded with coal, lime, feedstuffs and a couple of hay-making machines, as it wound its way through the 'heather-capped' Cambrian mountains reminds us of a railway and a world which has now long gone. One is more than aware that the goods guard on a service like this was not merely travelling through the countryside but was also part of it, waving to farm workers in the fields. Evans further asserted that one of the indispensable prerequisites of his job was the ability to be a 'good talker' and 'the possessor of reliable information on a variety of subjects'.

At each station the guard worked as part of a team with

station staff, dropping off wagons. He also helped supervise shunting them into the correct sidings and worked with shunters, porters or goods-shed staff to position wagons next to a crane so that goods could be quickly and easily unloaded. As the goods train progressed down the line it shrank appreciably, so that by the time it reached the final station, Llanfyllin, it consisted only of a few empty wagons and the guard's van. While the pick-up goods made its way along its timetabled route station staff would be busy unloading and loading wagons and shunting them into the correct order, ready for when the train returned later in the day. At smaller stations staff would have to rely on horsepower to help shunt wagons, as many did not have a steam locomotive regularly stabled. The horse also served as the means of delivering freight arriving at the station to customers.

The process of shunting in goods yards was not without incident or danger, as already mentioned. A Great Western accident report from 1944 illustrates this only too vividly.[18] A mishap at the yard at Cirencester caused by poor shunting led to an employee of one of the coal merchants there, one Henry Blackwell, having a close shave when two wagons crashed into the coal wagon he was unloading. Such was the speed of the wagons, Blackwell reported, that he did not have enough time to jump from his wagon and so received severe bruising to his arm, requiring him to take time off work. The Company admitted that the brakes on the offending wagons had not been correctly pinned down. While the sum paid in compensation was not revealed, the result could clearly have been much more serious.

Another important task carried out by staff at smaller stations, particularly those in rural areas, was the loading and unloading of livestock. The unloading of horses required great care, since they were a valuable commodity and could often be temperamental and thus difficult to handle. Some idea of the importance of this traffic can be gleaned from the fact that three pages are devoted to the correct loading and unloading of horses in the General Appendix to the Rule Book, which warned staff that 'if a horse is found to be restive from nervousness or any cause and there is a doubt of its travelling safely, the attention of the stationmaster must be drawn to it';[19] compensation claims for injury to such animals could cost the Company dear. The loading of these beasts could also be hazardous to staff, as a letter written in 1941 by a Mr S. Lyford, a member of staff at Didcot, reveals. Engaged in loading horses on 14 November, he and another porter, Mr A. Bennett, 'were about to close the flap of the horsebox when the horse nearest to the outside stepped back on to the flap, causing it to fall on Bennett's left foot'![20]

Left:
An official Company photograph
of a guard's uniform, taken in 1922.
National Railway Museum

Right:
An unidentified passenger guard
in British Railways days. Note the
flower in his buttonhole.

Below:
A Freight Train Journal, dating from
the 1940s, which was filled in by the
guard during each journey.

G.W.R.—FREIGHT TRAIN JOURNAL.

TRAIN No.
(Not to be filled in by Guard).

(368-1A) **F** G.W.R.

..................m. Freight Train from........................to........................on ....day........................194.......
(FOR FULL INSTRUCTIONS IN MAKING OUT THIS JOURNAL, SEE CIRCULAR No. 4820, DATED JANUARY, 1935).

HEADLAMPS	Actual time of		Late away from Station	Overtime at Station	Lost by Eng.	Account of whole time occupied by :—					Actual Number of Wagons (exclusive of Brake Van)										Actual No. of Wagons on Departure (exclusive of Brake Van)				Distance Miles (Not to be filled in by Guard)	Remarks as to Detentions at Stations and in running ; when Shunted for Trains to pass, give description and times of Trains which pass and Particulars of all Wagons over 10 tons capacity and General Remarks, etc.
						Shunting	Stati'n Truck Work	Stand'g at Signals Trains Ahead	Wait-ing for Trains to pass	Other Causes	TAKEN ON				PUT OFF				LOADED					
	Arrival	Departure									Class			Emp-ties	Class			Emp-ties	Class			Emp-ty		
STATIONS	H.	M.	H.	M.	H.	M	H.	M.	Mins.	Mins.	Mins.	Mins.	Mins.	Mins.	1	2	3		1	2	3		1	2	3			

LATE ARRIVAL		H.	M.	TOTALS																		TOTAL DISTANCE MILES		

LIVESTOCK, LOADED AND EMPTY TANK WAGONS CONVEYED, DEFECTIVE OR CRIPPLED WAGONS DETACHED EN ROUTE, GIVING STATIONS FROM AND TO.

State of Weather during journey ; if Wet, Frost, Fog or Snow and between what points.

Total time occupied in Division, including all Stops.
To be filled in by Guard.

	Hours	Minutes

BRAKE VAN.						TIMES RUN.	JOURNALS SENT.
No.	Home Station					Not to be filled in by Guard.	

30,000—B.M. 10. 1946. (8) S.

A short but interesting article in the Company magazine provides an insight into the goods work done by staff at small country stations in 1939. Based at Boxford station on the Lambourn Valley line, 61-year-old porter C. H. Brown described how, as the only member of staff at the station, he was responsible for passengers and goods and, between trains, for dealing with correspondence and delivering parcels and goods within the village. Dealing with goods traffic involved checking-in wagons that had arrived on the daily goods train and advising customers that their consignments had arrived at the station and were ready for collection. It was also his job to load wagons, wherein he demonstrated skill in the roping and sheeting of loads. Brown remarked that many other railwaymen might consider his job dull; he, however, did not, as, apart from meeting the trains and their passengers, he dealt with many other people in the course of his work, be they villagers, farm hands or carriers delivering and collecting goods from the yard.

Right:
Another service offered by the Company and dealt with by the Goods Department. This poster dates from the 1930s.

Below:
Using a 'scotch' to ease a wagon along the track.

2

The Traffic Department

Although the Goods Department generated more income for the Great Western Railway, it was always seen as the poor relation to the more glamorous passenger side of the operation. The latter was presided over by the grandly titled 'Superintendent of the Line' — one of the most important men on the railway. His responsibility it was to ensure that the railway was operated safely, expeditiously and profitably. Within the railway itself the longer title carried by its head was shortened to the 'Traffic Department', and this title probably described its job better. During the 1930s almost 18,000 staff were employed in the department, being responsible for the movement of passengers, parcels and goods, although, as we have seen, the handling and delivery of the latter were the responsibility of the Goods Department.

The Traffic Department staff included station staff, a large group that embraced porters, ticket collectors, stationmasters and other supervisory and parcels staff. Shunters, goods guards and passenger guards, whose work was described in Chapter 1, were also managed by the Traffic Department. The final group of staff who ensured the safe conveyance of passengers on the railway were the signalmen, who in 1935 numbered over 4,300. In addition, there were a considerable number of administrative staff employed in the Superintendent of the Line's office at Paddington.

The bureaucracy needed to run the passenger side of the operation was vast. Quite apart from the enormous task of recruiting, managing and paying the staff, the Traffic Department had to produce both public timetables and more detailed working timetables for its workforce. In this connection, it was the responsibility of the Department to ensure that passenger and freight stock were in the right locations at the right times, in order that other departments (such as the Locomotive Department) could operate services as advertised. The Traffic Department also fixed fares, printed and distributed tickets to stations, dealt with passenger complaints and administered the Company's parcels service. The Superintendent of the Line also managed the Publicity Department, noted for its eye-catching posters, books and other imaginative marketing work. Finally, the Traffic Department was responsible for railway safety on the GWR network and as such dealt with the rules, regulations and legislation as well as the investigation of accidents on the Company's lines.

In its publicity the GWR once boasted that it was the 'line of a thousand stations' — a claim which in all probability did not really stand up to close scrutiny, since the total probably included some very small halts and platforms, most of which hardly deserved the title of 'station'! Nevertheless, the Company's investment in its passenger facilities was substantial: it owned and maintained many large and imposing stations, the largest employing hundreds of staff and dealing with millions of passengers every year. Paddington, the Company's largest station, had in 1933 a complement of 1,389 staff, costing the Company over £225,000 per year in wages alone; in the same year it issued more than 1½ million tickets, and income from the station, including parcels revenue, totalled nearly £2,000,000.

No other GWR station really came close to Paddington's totals, although Birmingham Snow Hill, with a staff of 351 and an annual income of £446,188, was probably its nearest rival. Away from the larger regional stations the numbers of staff employed were more modest, albeit still generous by the standards of today. An example of a middle-sized station was that at Oxford, which had a staff of 189 in 1933, matched by annual takings of just over £150,000. Down the line towards Didcot, the much smaller wayside station of Culham still employed 10 staff, costing the Company almost £1,268 per year, even though total receipts were just £1,869 — a modest profit of £601 per annum.[1]

Whatever the size of the station, the man in charge — the stationmaster — was the most important, being responsible for its management and safe operation. One writer described the role as being 'to know everything about everybody, and to instruct everybody about everything'.[2] The job was all-encompassing and involved not only management of the staff but also responsibility for the safe and efficient working of the station. The position carried much weight both inside and outside the Company, and the stationmaster had considerable status in the community served by the railway, emphasising the importance of the station to a town or village for its livelihood, employment and convenience — a situation not prevalent today. Writing in 1939, Mr H. W. Carter, Stationmaster at Henley-on-Thames, reflected that he and his team would 'make a strong point of keeping on the very best of terms with the townspeople. It helps them and it is a good thing for us — as our rising receipts show!'[3]

The role of the stationmaster as manager was also important, as he supervised a workforce comprising porters, shunters, clerks and parcels staff and delivery drivers.

Discipline was, as always, strict; writing as early as 1905 Edward Hadley, the editor of the *Great Western Railway Magazine*, argued that the stationmaster was held responsible for 'the faithful and efficient discharge of the duties devolving upon all the Company's servants employed at his station'. It was his job, he continued, to ensure that no staff were 'idle' and his duty 'to comport himself in such a way as will lead his men to respect his authority'. When staff transgressed, and he needed to administer a rebuke, he should possess a 'dignity of manner, firmness of speech and the piercing eye that looks right through the delinquent'.[4] Certainly, in photographs most stationmasters of the period look stern and well able to deliver the rebuke noted by Hadley. It is interesting, however, to read the comments

Paddington, seen here in the 1920s, was the headquarters of the Traffic Department and by far the largest station on the system. *National Railway Museum*

At the other end of the scale, this unidentified station (possibly in West Somerset) is an example of the GWR's many small, rural outposts.

made by H. W. Carter over 30 years later, when he noted that he believed in giving his staff at Henley 'every encouragement' and that, as a consequence, 'we work as a team and … the day's work is all the more enjoyable for that'.[5]

The constant movement of staff working their way through the Great Western system meant that in some ways the stationmaster could be seen as the schoolteacher of the railway. Inevitably, most junior staff beginning their careers as lad porters or junior clerks would want to progress through the grades, and it was the stationmaster who began that schooling, instructing them on the basics of station work. Sid Keates, interviewed in 1997, remembered his first stationmaster — at Cirencester, where he began his career in the 1920s — as being a 'true railwayman'. He recalled being somewhat in awe of the 'little man who knew the rules end to end' although ultimately found him 'stern but sympathetic' to the young porter new to the job.

Like policemen, many stationmasters had a daily 'beat' to work. Having begun the day by opening correspondence and passing on any to be dealt with by clerks, they would start their round by inspecting the gas and water meters, before touring the station proper. Walking down the platform, they would visit waiting rooms and ticket offices and check that all posters and publicity were up to date. Another important check was that of the lavatories, to ensure that they were clean and presentable. The stationmaster would also climb the steps of the signalbox, to check that all was well with the signalman and to sign the Train Register summarising the punctuality of trains run the previous day.

At larger stations the stationmaster had additional help in such duties in the form of inspectors who acted as his 'eyes and ears'. One such inspector was George Rochester, whose retirement — after 52 years' service — was recorded in May 1911. Born in Basingstoke, he had begun his career on the Great Western Railway as a lad porter at Reading, before moving to Swindon Junction in 1862. Unlike many staff, who achieved promotion by moving around the network from station to station, Rochester appears to have been fortunate to remain at Swindon for virtually all his career.

Above:
Master of all he surveys.
An unidentified stationmaster,
believed to be at a station on the
Great Western / Great Central
joint line.

Left:
A wonderfully evocative view of the
staff of an unidentified Wiltshire
station. The stationmaster is seated
on the left.

The stationmaster at Weston-super-Mare, pictured in August 1960.

For the last 38 years of his working life he was employed as an Inspector, the final 16 being as Chief Inspector. Like most railway staff with such long experience, he remembered his contact with Royalty most vividly; as the most important man on the station, barring the stationmaster himself, he dealt with virtually all the important visitors, and spoke with pride about all the distinguished visitors he had helped. He recalled particularly the occasion when he was asked to supervise arrangements when Queen Victoria made a stop at Swindon on the way back from a trip to Bristol, in order that her daughter Princess Louise could make a trip to Cirencester. He remembered proudly that 'that incident brought me into very close touch with the Queen, in fact I conversed with her and escorted the Princess . . . into the saloon carriage prepared for her'.[6]

Stationmasters were responsible for what we would now call Health & Safety, and it was their duty on occasions to deal with painful and upsetting situations, particularly fatal accidents. Inspector Rochester recalled that in the late 1890s he had had the grisly task of dealing with an accident involving the previous stationmaster, Mr Bonner, who had a special ticket allowing him to ride on the footplate of the locomotive on a journey from Bristol to attend a meeting. Unfortunately, for some reason Bonner fell off the engine shortly before the train arrived at the station, and the inspector and staff from the station were forced to walk up the tracks with their hand lamps illuminating the way in the darkness until they discovered the dead body of the unfortunate stationmaster.

For both inspectors and stationmasters, if duties permitted it, a major responsibility would be to meet incoming train services and to see off departing trains. In the case of a smaller station like Henley, Stationmaster Carter was able to do this, even checking that all doors were properly closed before leaving. The stationmaster was ultimately responsible to Paddington for the prompt running of services and could be called to explain why train services were late, in much the same way that engine drivers and guards were.

With all his experience, the weight of expectation on a stationmaster was high; one writer thought that the job meant he 'should be, and must be a walking encyclopædia'. This extended not only to a thorough knowledge of the passenger timetables, to answer public enquiries, but also to knowledge of all the rules, regulations and routines adopted by the Company! Most people, the same writer noted, 'are both surprised and disgusted if they ask the stationmaster a question he cannot answer'.[7]

In the absence of Railway Police, who tended only to be employed at larger stations like Paddington, Bristol or Birmingham, the stationmaster was responsible for security on his station. At an unidentified station in one of the Welsh valleys one very observant stationmaster noticed that two miners, travelling on season tickets, always brought a pigeon with them as they came to work, releasing it as they walked

from the station to the pit head. This curious routine, repeated day after day, eventually made the stationmaster suspicious, and one morning he borrowed a gun, and brought the pigeon down, only to find two season tickets attached to its leg! The matter came to a head later in the day when two miners arrived without tickets; it then transpired that four miners were working two by two, on different shifts, and were using two pigeons to ensure that they all had tickets at the right time of the day, the second bird flying between the miners' homes and the pit to provide them with tickets for the return journey!

If the stationmaster stood at the top of the Traffic Department in terms of importance, the job of porter was probably near the bottom. Once described as the 'foundation stone of the Great Western Railway', the porter had responsibilities as many and varied as the stationmaster's, although probably involving far more hard graft! In general, the duties of porters at smaller country stations were rather more varied than those at larger establishments, where job descriptions were more rigid and supervision was tighter. One such summary of what the Company called a 'Grade 2' porter at Lavington station in Wiltshire notes that duties should include meeting trains and 'assisting with the work of the station'. More specifically, he was to 'clean station premises, including offices, windows, lavatories, platform lamps, footbridges etc' and was further expected to collect tickets and carry out 'bill-posting' — the upkeep and replacement of advertising and timetable posters on the station noticeboards.

The memories of Sid Keates provide a good summary of the porter's duties as outlined in the Lavington job description. Sid had begun his career at Cirencester station, where he picked up the rudiments of the job; he recalled the fact that the work was incredibly varied, especially when he was transferred to the smaller station at Minety & Ashton Keynes on the Swindon–Gloucester line. When he worked there the staff complement was only seven, and his duties thus included working in the goods yard as well as the station proper. The main area of responsibility was, of course, dealing with passengers. This included opening and unlocking the station when starting work in the morning, issuing tickets in the booking office and keeping the platforms and waiting rooms clean. A less popular duty was cleaning the toilets, as was the dirty job of lighting and maintaining the coal fires during the winter months.

The official uniform of a stationmaster at a large station. At a few large locations, such as Paddington and Birmingham, the holder of the office also wore a top hat on special occasions!

The station at Chipping Campden, in Gloucestershire. Note the well-maintained gardens on the platform.

As well as sweeping the platforms, porters were expected to help with the gardening; many stations had prize-winning gardens and keenly contested the annual Best Kept Station Garden competitions organised by the Great Western. Sid Keates also dealt with parcels traffic at the station, as well as more unusual arrivals such as that of pigeon traffic, which in the steam era was a substantial source of income for the railway. When the pigeons arrived at the station, staff released them and then made a charge for the return of the empty baskets. The first time he was asked to carry out this task Sid forgot to charge the 4d due on each hamper, thereby incurring the wrath of the stationmaster!

Sid was not charged for the lost revenue, but there were ways in which staff could supplement their income. Minety was a rural station with some well-heeled passengers and customers, and Sid remembered with pleasure the day when a local Colonel arrived to collect two cases of wine that had been delivered by rail to the station. When he arrived some of the more senior staff were on their lunch break, so Sid carried the boxes to the car. For his trouble he received a

A GWR examination certificate for station arrangements and goods accounting, awarded in 1928.

Above: One of the tasks least liked by staff at stations of all sizes was the unloading of full milk churns, which were heavy and awkward to handle. This scene was recorded at Paddington.

Below: At larger stations charges were made for porters working off the premises. This 19th-century notice outlines the arrangements at Ealing.

425.

GREAT WESTERN RAILWAY.

SCALE OF CHARGES

AUTHORISED TO BE MADE BY

OUTSIDE PORTERS

FOR DELIVERY OF LUGGAGE AND PARCELS

TO AND FROM EALING STATION.

Luggage Parcel or Parcels delivered at same place:—

	Not exceeding ¼ u mile.	Every additional ¼ of a mile.
If not exceeding 14 lbs. in all............................	3d.	1d.
14 lbs. and not exceeding 56 lbs.	4d.	1½d.
56 lbs. „ 112 lbs.	6d.	2d.
112 lbs. „ 4 cwt.	8d.	3d.

Any quantity of Luggage or Parcels exceeding 4 cwt. to be by special agreement, not to exceed 2d. per cwt. for first ¼ of a mile, and 1d. per cwt. for every additional ¼ of a mile.

☞ When detained more than ¼ hour loading or unloading, for every additional ¼ hour .... 3d.

One-half more in addition to above charges to be made after 8 p.m. from November 1st to March 1st, and after 10 p.m. during the other months.

PADDINGTON, *June,* 1896.   BY ORDER.

2s 6d tip — a substantial sum — much to the chagrin of his older colleagues. Working at a station in a rural area had other compensations; at Christmas, staff received turkeys or pheasants from grateful customers. The owner of the public house opposite the station supplied staff with alcohol on occasions, and Sid remembered receiving a half bottle of whisky, even though at that time he did not drink anything so strong!

One situation which still irritated Sid Keates even 70 years on was the fact that after 6pm and on Saturday afternoons the station was left in the sole charge of the porter on duty. The stationmaster worked only a half-day on Saturday, and the clerk did not work at all, so from lunchtime onwards

Sid's job was 'sheer murder'! Saturdays were the busiest day of the week, particularly as the Company offered cheap day returns from Minety to Swindon for 1s 6d. Worse still were the days when Swindon Town Football Club played at home, for demand for special 'Football returns' at 1s was very high. As well as coping with all the additional passengers, staff would have to cope on their own with any other parcels or goods work. Sid always felt that staff should have been paid an additional sum for the extra responsibility, but, since any complaint to a higher authority — namely the Divisional Office at Gloucester — would have to be addressed through the stationmaster himself, he had to carry on regardless!

Another of Sid Keates' duties was to look after the station clock, situated above one of the fireplaces in the waiting room. It was Sid's job to wind it once a week, although he remembered having to stand on a chair to reach it! In the early 20th century a telegraph signal was transmitted from Paddington once a week at a pre-arranged time, to enable all clocks in the system to be properly regulated. At larger stations, with numerous public clocks, the job of clock-winding would have been more substantial and would most likely not have been entrusted to a junior porter. If time-pieces were losing time or malfunctioned, they would be sent by train to the Signal Works at Reading, where clockmakers maintained Great Western clocks in a special workshop.

Staff working at smaller stations were expected to help as required with the handling, loading and unloading of goods in the yard or the goods shed. Sid Keates remembered the hard work required to unload the box vans that were shunted into the shed most days. Wagons from locations as diverse as Paddington, South Lambeth and Plymouth had to be dealt with quickly and reloaded ready for the next goods train to pick them up. The rural location of the station also meant that there were numerous deliveries of livestock. A nearby dealer, Mr Frank Reed, brought much business to the station, in terms of deliveries to and from the yard. Sid recalled that he helped load many calves for transit elsewhere and that the canny livestock dealer gave the

frisky young animals bottles of stout to keep them quiet! On another occasion the peace of the small station yard was shattered by a delivery of eight wagonloads of sheep from Scotland. Sid confessed that he had never seen so many sheep in one place at one time!

At larger stations porters had nothing like the level of responsibility enjoyed by Sid Keates; as he noted, their main duties were to meet, supervise and despatch trains and to keep the platforms and waiting rooms clean. At busy locations this could be a thankless task, as passengers often got on the wrong trains, mislaid their luggage or arrived too late to catch their intended train. Platform staff naturally bore the brunt of passengers' frustration and responded with varying levels of professionalism. Sid's first stationmaster insisted that staff should be 'smart, clean and polite' — an instruction to which most Great Western porters adhered.

The job of a porter was by its nature one which was physically taxing. Quite apart from the effort of being on one's feet virtually all day on an eight-hour shift, there was a good deal of lifting and carrying to be done. As well as passenger luggage, there were deliveries and parcels to be dealt with. When Joe Hill retired at Swindon Junction station in 1951, one of his old colleagues, unable to attend his retirement party, wrote describing some of the characteristics needed by a porter. The mention of Joe's name, Mr S. G. Walker noted, brought 'a picture of heavy engine piston boxes being raised and dashed from parcel vans with Herculean strength'. The porters who worked under his direction were expected to demonstrate similar qualities, he continued, 'and often a box on the ear or dig in the ribs was given with this object in view'.[8]

One of the Great Western's principal aims was to

Inspector Joe Hill, on his retirement at Swindon Junction station in 1951. *Ian & Jane Hill*

A GWR ticket-collector at work at Paddington in the 1940s.

maximise income and ticket sales. For this reason, at larger stations not only were there porters, who could check passengers' tickets, but also ticket-collectors employed specifically to examine, punch and collect the card Edmondson tickets then used. Most stations were closed stations, in that passengers were not allowed onto the platform without a valid ticket for travel; if a member of the public were seeing off a friend or relative, he or she needed to purchase a platform ticket before passing through the ticket barrier. An instruction issued by the Superintendent of the Line in 1938 urged stationmasters to adopt 'every reasonable means in their power to ensure that passengers do not join trains at stations without first having taken tickets, and they are requested to impress the importance of this on the Ticket Collecting and other staff under their supervision'.[9] The circular gave details of scams and tricks being practised by dishonest travellers and further instructed staff to try to note the class of the carriage from which passengers alighted, to be sure they had the correct ticket. This would have been very difficult at a busy station like Paddington! Problems also arose over the issuing of 'excess' tickets for those passengers

who either did not have a ticket or had changed their travel plans *en route*. 'Care should be taken as far as possible,' the circular noted, 'to obtain confirmation of a passenger's statement as to the starting point of the journey when excess is being received from a passenger who has no ticket.' If necessary, ticket-collectors were to speak to the guard to obtain confirmation. Staff were also warned to check the lavatories after the departure of the train, to ensure that fare-dodgers had not hidden there, and were further urged not to leave ticket barriers or gates open or unlocked at quiet times and so allow dishonest passengers either to alight without tickets or to retain tickets for reuse!

Being in such close contact with passengers, the ticket-collector did far more than merely punch tickets; as Mr G. Mitchell, a ticket-collector at the busy seaside resort of Dawlish, reported, his job was also to serve as 'an information bureau', especially at the height of the season, when there were crowds of holidaymakers wanting to know train departure times, arrival times and details of connections. In the winter, however, many of his customers were 'regulars . . . about whom I know almost everything,

including their usual trains and most of their peculiar requirements'.[10] Mitchell was sometimes called upon to deputise for what became known as 'travelling ticket inspectors', who walked through the compartments and corridors of trains as they sped through the West Country, ensuring that travellers had the correct ticket for their journey.

At the end of most station platforms was a signalbox. Signalmen were also employees of the Traffic Department, and their sometimes lonely job was nevertheless one of the most important on the railway, as they were responsible for trains and thus also for passengers. At its height the Great

Western Railway had almost 1,900 signalboxes and ground frames used to control signals and points. The first 'boxes had appeared in 1863, replacing the primitive arrangements that had existed before. In the early days of the railway, policemen controlled the passage of trains from one section of the line to another by hand-operating the signals themselves and using a time-interval system to ensure that services ran safely from station to station. The invention of the telegraph and the 'block system' allowing trains to be signalled safely from one section of line to another led to the construction of signalboxes, which housed both the telegraph instruments (later known as 'block' instruments)

Claverdon signalbox just after completion in 1910. *National Railway Museum*

and the levers to control the semaphore signals and point-work. It is not intended here to give any great detail on the mechanics or working of the Great Western signalling system, as this has been admirably chronicled elsewhere, most notably by Adrian Vaughan in his *Pictorial Record of Great Western Signalling*.[11] What is hoped, however, is to give the reader something of a feeling of the life and working conditions experienced by signalmen in the steam era.

For those wishing to become a signalman, there were a number of ways in to the job. For some, the route to a position in a signalbox was by becoming a lad porter, as Sid Keates had done. Being a porter gave staff an excellent introduction to the railway way of life and a general grounding in the rules and regulations that were so much a part of the job. Sid became interested in the job when spending time in the 'box at Minety, learning from the signalman on duty.

The next stage was to become a signalman porter, which combined the two jobs, usually at smaller rural locations

with little traffic, before becoming a signalman proper. Mr J. S. Cotterill, who (like many in this book) spent his entire career on the railway, began his working life in this way, starting in 1911 as a lad porter at Hagley in the West Midlands before moving to Hampton Loade on the Severn Valley line three years later as a signalman porter. He worked his way through various 'boxes during the course of World War 1, having been refused permission to enlist in the armed forces. Writing in 1915, the Divisional Superintendent at Worcester informed him that, despite his admirable desire to join up, a large number of staff had already been given permission to do so and that it was in the national interest that the railways continued to run efficiently, in order to move troops and munitions. The Superintendent concluded: 'With some reluctance, therefore, it has had to be decided in your case that permission cannot be given, and it is hoped . . . you will appreciate that you are serving your country by remaining at your post, notwithstanding the very natural desire to do so in another way.'[12] The shortage of trained signal staff probably saved Cotterill's life; given the slaughter on the Western Front, his chances of survival would have been limited. After the war he moved to Bristol, eventually becoming a 'relief' signalman deputising for staff that were off sick or on holiday. This naturally led him eventually to become an Inspector before retiring in 1960.

A more direct route to the signalman's job was to start as a booking boy or 'lad telegraphist'. K. Wixey began his career as a signalman this way, joining the Company just before Nationalisation, in 1946.[13] Having passed the customary medical, he started work at Cheltenham Lansdown Junction 'box, where his principal duty was to maintain the Train Register. At larger signalboxes, where signalmen were kept busy operating the block instruments and signal levers, boys were employed to record the time and details of each train movement passing the 'box. This was no mean feat; in his description of the large signalbox at Exeter West Junction, Adrian Vaughan notes that keeping a minute-by-minute record not only of train movements but also of the various block bell codes sent and received was more remarkable than the operation of the lever frame itself. What was more remarkable still, he continued, was how quickly (within months) 15-year-old booking boys could learn the intricacies of complicated signalboxes and cope with the pressures of busy summer Saturdays, when hundreds of trains could be dealt with during a shift. Adrian cites as an example the summer of 1956, when, in one hour, 22 trains were scheduled to pass the 'box — a total that did not include shunting movements or any extra trains that could be squeezed in.[14]

As well as keeping the Train Register up to date, the booking boy would be responsible for answering the telephone and relaying messages to the signalman. When the pressure was off, his other main job was keeping the 'box clean. A characteristic of Great Western and British Railways Western Region signalboxes was that invariably they were spotlessly clean; K. Wixey remembered mopping out the linoleum floor at least twice a week and spending time cleaning the windows, of which there were naturally a good many. The signal levers themselves were also kept clean and the steel handles burnished; so as not to mark the steel, signalmen always used a cloth to grip the handle when 'pulling off' a signal. The cast-iron treads between the levers could be polished with black lead paste, which was also applied to the stove in the 'box. Much of the cleaning was done on the night shift or on Sundays, when traffic might be lighter.

For young staff, training was largely 'on the job'. By watching more senior staff, listening and being allowed to operate equipment under supervision, they gradually gained confidence in the running of a 'box and the rules and procedures for performing this task. In the early 20th

One of the duties of a junior member of staff, usually a lad porter or a signalman porter, was to check and maintain all the long-burning oil lamps at the station. This would involve climbing up the signal posts to remove lamps' interiors and carrying them around the site using this ingenious wooden handle.

century the Company set up signalling schools at a number of locations, using a printed synopsis of the *Course of Instruction on the subject of the Safe Working of Railways*. The 1924 edition of this book noted that it was for the benefit of those attending signalling classes and 'also for the assistance of those members of staff who, although not able to attend a class, are desirous of qualifying by means of a correspondence course'. Before progressing, signalmen would be examined by District Inspectors who would test their knowledge of procedures, rules and regulations.

The size and location of the signalbox determined the pressure under which signal staff worked, since a busy 'box like that at Exeter West (already briefly described) was a very different place from a smaller 'box on a branch line. Writing

Above: The interior of Reading signalbox. The booking boy is seated on the right, answering the telephone as well as completing the Train Register. *National Railway Museum*

Below: The spotless interior of Pontypool Road signalbox, pictured in 1961. *National Railway Museum*

Right:
The signalman leans out of the window of Colwall 'box on a hot August afternoon in 1964.

Below:
Didcot North 'box, seen in 1964.

Signalman Pullen at Chipping Campden in 1967 after winning a British Railways Safety competition. Behind him can be seen the wheel for operating the level-crossing gates.

in the *Great Western Railway Magazine* in 1938, signalman T. H. Light, who worked in the 'box at Llandebie in West Wales, gave an account of his working day. Not all 'boxes on quieter lines operated continuously, and he began his shift at 4am. His first task was to test the block instruments by sending the opening code to the signalboxes on either side of him. He then checked the lever frame itself, ensuring that all signals and points were working correctly, for, if this were not the case, a 'line man' would be needed to operate the points manually until they could be repaired — a complicated operation. More serious problems would involve 'pilot working', whereby a member of staff would ride on locomotives between stations to ensure that trains passed safely from one section to the other.

The 'box worked by Signalman Light had the additional complication of a level crossing to operate. Having opened the 'box, on winter mornings, staff would descend the steps from the 'box to light the lamps on the crossing gates. Signalmen encountered problems in the Blackout, and an accident report from 1944 illustrates the impact the Blackout had. The Great Western received a claim for £9 5s from the Worcestershire Constabulary for an accident that occurred at Oldbury & Langley Green. A police officer, one Sgt Hawkins, was riding his bicycle when the signalman, not seeing the cyclist in the murk of a wet January evening, shut his level-crossing gates without warning, knocking the unfortunate sergeant to the ground and giving him a bruised leg. The Company was ordered to pay compensation to the police because the signalman had not shouted a warning as stipulated. However, as the usual oil lamps on the gates had been removed for the duration of the war, such an accident was almost inevitable!

In a small 'box the signalman himself was responsible for completing the Train Register, as well as for various other duties, including the cleaning. One of the most important was to check the train as it passed, not only for its general condition but also, most importantly, as to whether it had a tail lamp. If this were missing, the train couplings might have parted and some of the train might be stranded in the section without its locomotive or (if the line were on a gradient) running away. If the 'box were on a single-line section, the signalman would also be responsible for the operation of the electric train staff, and at each 'box the signalman and driver or fireman would exchange tokens allowing trains to proceed safely from one stretch of line to the other.

One of the greatest concerns for signal staff related to bad weather, which might affect the operation of the 'box, signals or points. The effects of cold weather on the operation of the railway will be described in a later chapter. The greatest worry was fog, and, if visibility deteriorated sufficiently, the signalman could call in fog signalmen, who would stand at the side of the track and signal trains through sections using flags. Fog signalmen also used detonators — small explosive devices which could be placed on the track and which emitted a loud bang when run over by trains. These were also used to indicate that signals were not working and to warn of danger, being used also by guards in emergency situations to protect trains that had broken down. Detonators could also be used for other purposes; a notice issued in 1951 to enginemen at Bristol warned staff not to misuse detonators, following an accident (at an unnamed station) whereby staff had exploded detonators and sounded whistles to celebrate the marriage of a colleague; unfortunately the driver of a passenger train had set off without checking the signals, and more detonators laid by the signalman to try and stop the train colliding with a goods train ahead had been ignored by the crew, who thought that they were part of the wedding celebrations![15]

Right:
An example of a much smaller 'box, at St Mary's Crossing, near Stroud.

Below:
The fireman of GWR '14xx' 0-4-2T No 1473 reaches out to take the single-line token at Aylesbury South.

The more remote signalboxes away from stations and depots sometimes lacked even basic staff facilities. Adrian Vaughan describes the 'box at Tigley, near Totnes. This was a small cabin with only nine levers, and staff there had no electricity, no running water and a 'lavatory' that was in a copse behind the 'box. Water for washing was obtained from a rainwater butt, whilst drinking water was usually delivered in a milk churn on the front buffer-beam of a banking engine which had worked to assist a freight train up the 1-in-47 gradient at Rattery; having completed this task, the crew would return light, calling at the 'box on the way back to Totnes.[16]

The stoves used in signalboxes were supplied with coal on a regular basis, but in winter there was often not enough to keep a stove burning all day and night. Signalmen often supplemented their meagre supply with the assistance of friendly locomotive staff, who helped where they could, despite management opposition. Proof of the existence of such unofficial arrangements comes in the form of a number

of memoranda that were issued by the Locomotive Department in 1952, following a dispute as to whether the crew of pannier tank No 9782 had given coal to the signalman at Taplow. The driver, based at Slough, denied that he had transferred coal, but one cannot help but think that railway solidarity was in operation between the crew and signalman! A few years later another notice was issued by Paddington: 'It has been brought to notice that station and signalbox staff have been supplied on occasion with coal from engine tenders. This practice is irregular and must cease forthwith.'

For an impression of a signalman's working day in a busier 'box, the account given by E. O. Jones, who worked at Ardley in the West Midlands, provides a useful summary. Writing in 1938, Jones described his job as a test of nerve and ability, for the safety and punctuality of Great Western services depended on him. He noted that his 'box had 54 levers, block instruments, bell tappers, signal arm, lamps and lock repeaters, a telephone and — last but not least — a stove on which 'many a tasty breakfast has been cooked!' [17]

Beginning his shift, Jones would exchange notes with the man who had been on 'night turn' before signing the Train Register and checking the equipment. Attention was paid to the repeaters — instruments on the block shelf which showed, for example, the position of signals which were out of sight of the 'box — or lamp repeaters, which showed whether or not signal lamps were burning. He would also check to see if there were any new Special Train Notices or other circulars that needed attention. With the approach of a train, he would receive the 'Call Attention' bell signal from the 'box in the rear, which he would promptly acknowledge. Following this, another signal, this time asking 'Is Line Clear?' would be given in the correct bell code, according to the type of train approaching. For example, an express passenger service would be indicated by four beats of the bell, while a freight train would be signalled by a bell code of 3-4-1. There were bell codes for every eventuality, perhaps the most important being 4-4-4, which indicated a Royal Train. If the line were clear, and signals and points set, the signalman would accept the train by repeating the signal, at the same time placing the block instrument to 'Line Clear'. This action transmitted to the 'box in the rear, and the train now approached the 'box, which then sent a 'Train Entering Section' bell message. Once this was acknowledged, the block instrument would be moved to the 'Train On Line' position. As it passed, the train would be checked as described earlier, and, once it had passed a point $\frac{1}{4}$ mile beyond the home signal, a 'Train out of Section' message could be communicated to the 'box in the rear, allowing the next service to be accepted.

To the non-railwayman, the description given above may seem somewhat technical and complicated, but it serves to highlight that this was precisely the nature of the signalman's job. It was critical that he understand each bell and block-instrument signal and that he maintain control of the situation when trains were passing frequently and at high speed. A report in the *Swindon Evening Advertiser* of March 1957 described the scene at Swindon West 'box, where a reporter had spent a morning with staff. With 171 levers, this was one of the biggest on the Western Region and was situated at the west end of the station, close to the entrance to Swindon Works and to the junction between the main Bristol–London line and the Gloucester line. It was manned by two signalmen and a booking boy, working three shifts — 6am–2pm, 2pm–10pm and 10pm–6am. The reporter had rather naïvely assumed that pulling the signal levers would be a relatively simple task but soon found that this was not the case: although pulling the lever to move a nearby signal or point was easy, for signals that might be up to $\frac{1}{4}$ mile away the friction on the signal wires meant that strength and technique were required. (Retired signal staff argue moreover that there was a knack to pulling certain levers, which required more than just brute force!) Concluding his survey of the 'box, the unnamed reporter wrote that the signalman must ally 'a keen brain with good muscles'. [18]

An article written almost 40 years later in the same *Swindon Evening Advertiser* gave details of one of the first women in charge of a signalbox, in Wiltshire. This chapter has referred to 'signalmen', but during World War 2 women made inroads into the traditionally male preserve of the signalbox, and Mrs Victoria Head became a signalwoman in the winter of 1940. Told by a friend that there was a vacancy at a nearby 'box at Stratton, she went to the station to apply for the job. She was given two weeks' training at Bristol and a further week's training with a senior signalman at the 'box itself, after which she was left on her own. The 'box was situated on the Highworth branch line, and the line had a number of factories with sidings leading off the branch. Although Mrs Head left the railway after the war, she enjoyed her time on the job and had no problems with her male workmates. 'The men were nice,' she recalled. 'They kept asking me for dates and paid me a lot of attention!' [19]

Those who worked in signalboxes during the steam era still remember such times largely with fondness. What is clear today, however, is the very responsible position held by staff and their dedication to passenger safety. As one writer noted, the job of signalman was no sinecure, for one false move or mistake on his (or her) part could result in a serious or potentially fatal accident. The fact that so few accidents did occur is a tribute to their equipment, their training and their dedication to the job.

The Engine Shed

To many on and off the railway, the driver's job was seen as perhaps the 'premier' job — no other employee seemed to demand so much respect. Until recent times it was common for passengers to shake hands with the locomotive crew to congratulate them at the end of a run at Paddington, which would be somewhat unusual today! However, the driver on the footplate of a great express locomotive like *King George V* would have arrived at that position after a long apprenticeship through the 'grades', starting at the very bottom as an engine cleaner or 'call boy' and, although in a privileged position as a top-link driver, would have earned that role through a lot of hard and dirty work. From the bottom to the top could take 20 years, by modern standards an inordinate length of time, but in steam days this was seen as the best way to ensure that the driver

in charge of the 'Cornish Riviera Limited' was the cream of the crop! This chapter outlines the beginning of the journey for footplate staff — life in the shed as a cleaner.

Until the modern era, being an engine driver was the boyhood ambition of many children. The dream for Swindon driver Gordon Shurmer began in 1926, when he was given a Hornby tin-plate model locomotive by his father. Even today he clearly remembers sitting in a zinc bath at his home in Havelock Street, Swindon, and receiving the clockwork model as his present on his fifth birthday. From then on it was the only thing he wanted to do!

As was the case with many railway jobs, the pathway to a job on the footplate was eased by having a father or close relative already employed within the department. Harold Gasson was a good example of this tradition, both his father

Reading shed, pictured in the 1930s. *National Railway Museum*

A fine collection of Edwardian locomotives outside Worcester shed before World War 1.
National Railway Museum

A locomotive crew — Driver Gregory and Fireman Wilson — at Bristol Bath Road shed *c*1925.

and uncle being employed by the Great Western at Didcot and in the South Wales valleys. In his childhood years he had spent many hours in and around sheds and steam locomotives, and, as he wrote later, 'I had the time of my life and couldn't wait until I was officially old enough to join the Great Western'.[1] The official age for joining the Locomotive Department was 16, so, as most boys left school two years earlier in those days, most with ambitions of working on the footplate had to bide their time in a variety of other occupations.

It was not unusual for boys to join other departments of the railway after leaving school, with the aim of transferring when the time came. Despite only ever wanting to be an engine driver, Gordon Shurmer did not have an easy path to his lifetime ambition. His father worked for the Great Western as a boilermaker in the great railway works at Swindon, and numerous other relations were also employed there; however, he had no direct family on the footplate and remembers his father saying that he had about as much chance of becoming an engine driver as a 'snowflake in a baker's oven'.

In 1936 Gordon became an office boy at Swindon Works, pending an apprenticeship there. Eventually offered the choice of a trade as a boilermaker, coppersmith, tinsmith or painter, he arrived at the office of Mr Smith, Chief Draughtsman at the works. The windows of this office faced the Gloucester branch line and beyond that the smoky confines of Swindon locomotive shed. Pointing to the shed, Smith asked Gordon if he really wanted to do a dirty, filthy job which meant that he might be at work on Christmas Day, when he could be with his family, or on Sundays, when he should be at church, or at night, when everyone else was

fast asleep! The stern but clearly thoughtful official told him to go away and think about it. His father was still convinced that, despite his son's ambition, the security of a works apprenticeship was the right path, but Gordon returned the following Wednesday, as determined as ever to live his dream. Mr Smith asked Gordon what his decision was. 'Sir, I want to be an engine driver' was the reply. 'Then so you bloody shall!' came the response, and thus it was that Gordon began his career in the Locomotive Department of the Great Western Railway on 1 February 1937.

Others trod a somewhat different path on the way to joining the Locomotive Department. Born and bred in the West Midlands, like Gordon Shurmer, Tony Barfield only ever wanted to work on the railway; however, after his interview and medical examination he was judged as being underweight and slightly too small. His obvious enthusiasm and knowledge of locomotives nevertheless led to what would now be called a 'conditional' offer of employment. He was offered a job as a lad porter at Hagley, a small station close to Kidderminster, now on the preserved Severn Valley Railway. This job would, he was told, 'stretch your bones and put a bit of meat on you'.[2] After a few months, he was promised, he could start work in the shed.

Standing on the platform of Swindon station, waiting to travel back to the West Midlands, the disappointment Tony felt at not being able to begin his career in the locomotive shed was tempered by the fact that he would soon be a railway employee. In the next few months, as the most junior member of staff, he tackled the many and varied tasks which were part of life in a small country station. As well as keeping the platforms and waiting rooms clean and tidy, he helped unload cattle and deliver parcels around the village by bike. It was during this time that his railway career almost came to a sudden and fatal end, when a platform trolley got stuck as he was pushing it across a board crossing at the end of the platform. Engrossed in the task of freeing the trolley and retrieving the luggage trunks that had fallen from it, he failed to see that a train was fast approaching. Almost too late, he realised his predicament, freed the trunk and trolley and dived into the space between the platform and rails. The locomotive, 'Saint' No 2920 *Saint David*, came to a grinding halt, and he was hauled to safety, having had a very close shave! The driver of *Saint David*, having ascertained that all was well, turned and said to the petrified boy: 'Take my tip, boy: pack up this job and get yourself on to the footplate — it's much safer!' Within a few months, Tony had begun his career as an engine cleaner at Kidderminster shed!

Another Great Western driver, Tom Conduit, was brought up in South Wales. His father was a Company employee, working in the docks at Swansea and Llanelli. Tom himself had had a variety of jobs before becoming a cleaner, including spells in the Goods Department, on a farm and in various steel and tin works. By the time he was old enough to join the railway as a cleaner, in July 1941, he was living in Monmouth and so applied to the railway at Worcester, the nearest large depot. There does not seem to have been a completely uniform way in which junior staff were recruited; quite often, however, the process began with a preliminary interview at a depot, where boys were selected.

Beginning his career on the Great Western just after World War 1, Alf Summers, having been brought up in West London, applied to join the railway after working in both a factory and a chemist's shop. Unlike Gordon Shurmer, who had wanted to be an engine driver from a young age, Alf drifted into the profession almost by accident, inspired largely by another GWR driver who had lived in the flat above his family in Harlesden. This driver had agreed to sponsor him, and they were duly summoned to Old Oak Common shed for an interview, during which Alf was asked a series of questions including what he perceived to be the key one: 'Have you any relations working for the Great Western Railway?' Giving a negative answer to this question brought what Alf thought was a frown to one of the interviewers, and he left the room convinced that he had been rejected. Driver Flaxman, on whose recommendation he was being considered, was then called in to talk to the panel, and emerged after only a few minutes, reinforcing Alf's sense of unease. The news, however, was better than he

A view of Bristol Bath Road shed, where Tom Conduit spent part of World War 2 as a fireman, recorded some years earlier, in 1934.

'Castle' 4-6-0 No 5039 *Rhuddlan Castle* in the roundhouse at Old Oak Common shed in the 1950s.

could have hoped. Driver Flaxman told him: 'You have been selected to take your test and medical at Swindon. You will be sent for!'[3]

Whatever the method of selection for footplate staff, all were required to submit themselves for an examination at Swindon, and most remember the experience as a mixture of fear, anticipation and bewilderment. Potential applicants were issued with a free pass to Swindon, and arrived at the railway town most apprehensive about their prospects of passing what was seen as an onerous test process. The stream of young men getting off the train at Swindon Junction must have been a regular sight to staff there, and Tony Barfield remembered being told by one ticket-collector that he 'had the look of a railwayman', which helped ease some of the butterflies he was suffering! From the station, applicants walked along Station Road into London Street, through the heart of the Railway Village, passing the famous Tunnel Entrance to the Works. On the occasion of his interview Tony Barfield arrived just in time to hear the lunchtime Works hooter blowing and witnessed something of the hustle and bustle of Swindon in the steam era as hundreds of Works staff streamed out of the factory.

The workshops behind them, the new applicants walked past the GWR fire station in Bristol Street and along the side of the Railway Park until they reached their final destination, Park House. Dating from 1876, this imposing Gothic building faced onto the park and had originally been used as accommodation and consulting rooms for G. M. Swinhoe, the Chief Medical Officer employed by the Great Western Medical Fund Society, a health scheme set up for Works employees. With the expansion of the Medical Fund into new premises in the late 19th century, the building was converted and remained as the examination centre for the Great Western's Locomotive Department for well over 60 years.

The format for the examination of potential candidates for the Department appears to have changed little over the years. Writing about his first visit to Park House in the 1920s, Alf Summers described how, having followed the directions there, he found himself sitting in a waiting room with about 30 others of a similar age but from widely differing parts of the country. The accents and dialects varied from the (to him) familiar Cockney to Devon, Cornish and Welsh, among others. General knowledge, writing and arithmetic tests came first, followed by an eyesight test, clearly crucial for life on the footplate, where the correct spotting of lineside signals was essential. Harold Gasson described the conventional eyesight test, with first one eye then the other being checked, and remembered being then asked to look at a box of rather grubby strands of coloured wool. Candidates were asked to sort the wool into piles of the same colour — a primitive but effective method of ensuring that Great Western footplate staff were not colourblind! Gasson suspected that the wool he had sorted was probably that sorted by his father and guessed that the thousands of grubby fingers which had mauled it in the intervening 30 years had made the job of sorting it all the more difficult!

The final part of the test was a thorough medical examination. Quite how thorough this was can be gleaned from the experience of Alf Summers, who was told by the doctor examining him that he would not pass the test because one of his teeth was decayed; if a dentist were to

remove the tooth during the lunch break, he would be happy to pass him! Despite the fact that, upon further examination by the dentist, the tooth turned out to be completely normal, Alf Summers nevertheless had it extracted, and the gap in his mouth was enough to satisfy the doctor!

Having completed their ordeal, the applicants were told of their fate, and, if successful, no doubt idled back to the station with a light heart. The ever-perceptive staff at Swindon Junction, as well as identifying potential footplate candidates, could tell from their demeanour which candidates had passed the test. In his reminiscences, however, Alf Summers noted that, although he had been given very broad hints, he did not finally discover that he had passed until a few days later, when he received a letter from the Great Western Railway requesting him to report to Old Oak Common shed at 8am to begin his employment as an engine-cleaner.

Gordon Shurmer was brought firmly down to earth on his first morning. When he arrived at the office of the Swindon running shed at 9am Mr Duck, the Shed Foreman, told him: 'Young man, you're late! You are not working in the offices now'. The Foreman gave him a ticking-off, reminding him that cleaners on his shift began work an hour earlier, at 8am, and that from now on he would be working all hours! For 16-year-old starters, even those who had perhaps worked in factories or workshops, their introduction to life in the shed must have been a rude awakening. Steam, smoke, oil, grime, noise and bustle assailed the senses, and, even in the years after World War 2, conditions in engine sheds did not improve dramatically until the onset of dieselisation in the late 1950s. The overwhelming feeling in many larger sheds in the steam era was, however, the gloom, the smoke and steam belching from the locomotives being compounded by the gas lighting used until the 1950s.

In most depots drivers 'booked on' in the offices close to the entrance to the shed. This

Above:
Just how dirty shed life was can be seen from this picture of one of the shed staff looking in the smokebox of a 'Hall' 4-6-0.

Left:
Clearing ash from the smokebox of a 'Star' 4-6-0 locomotive in 1938.

Washing down the same 'Star' locomotive after having ash removed from its smokebox. The picture was taken at Bristol Bath Road shed.

normally involved shouting to the time clerk seated there that they had arrived. For the more junior members of staff things were more formal. To avoid the possibility of any 'funny business', staff were issued with brass 'checks' or tokens, handed in to the time clerk at the end of a shift, which recorded attendance that day. There is little doubt that at large sheds such a measure was entirely logical; Alf Summers noted that when he started work at Old Oak Common he was amazed when around 40 cleaners of all ages emerged from the cleaners' cabin at the beginning of his first shift. At this depot cleaners were divided into gangs of four, although this was not, of course, the case at smaller sheds, where cleaners often worked in pairs or singly.

The actual job of cleaning required the application of large quantities of 'elbow grease', for, by their nature and operation, steam locomotives were dirty. Cleaning an engine meant more than polishing the brass and copper that distinguished Great Western designs. The large areas of brightwork, which included the copper-capped chimney, brass safety-valve cover and polished name- and number-plates needed to be kept sparkling, especially on the engines used on the most important expresses, such as the 'Cornish Riviera Limited' and the 'Cheltenham Flyer'. Working at

Old Oak Common, Alf Summers noticed that engines used on the West of England main line, which ran along the Devon coast at Dawlish and Teignmouth, returned to the shed looking particularly weather-beaten and required extra work to remove the salt and grime from their paintwork. As he remarked, it was a fairly easy task to clean a nameplate like that of *Lode Star*, but engines with longer names, such as *Knight of the Golden Fleece* and *Isambard Kingdom Brunel* were hard work! The over-riding aim, however, was that, when an engine backed down the tangle of lines from Old Oak Common depot to Paddington station, ready to haul a crack express to the West, it did so in 'ex-works' condition. In Victorian times, such was the pride in the condition of engines that cleaners covered the large brass domes of engines such as the 'Achilles' 4-2-2 locomotives with sacking on their journey from the shed to the station, and this was not removed until the engine was at rest under the roof of Brunel's great terminus.

As well as polishing the brasswork of engines, cleaners had to tackle the much less pleasant job of keeping the wheels, motion and underside clean. For all the merits of the Great Western's locomotive designs, some were extremely difficult to work on, particularly when there was no pit to enable

Smokebox cleaning being scrutinised postwar by a 'Time & Motion' expert at Southall.

cleaners to gain access to the inside motion. An example of this was noted by Alf Summers, who told of the difficulties of climbing into an extremely tight space between the frames of a 'Star', in order to clean the back of the big ends. There was also a sandbox situated in the middle of the frame, and this and the space around it needed to be clean, as the driver or fireman would himself climb under the locomotive when oiling it prior to leaving the shed. As well as the inside motion, there were the outside motion and valve gear, buffers, wheels and frames to be cleaned.

One job not relished by cleaning staff was that of cleaning the locomotive firebox. This confined space, normally filled to the brim with the locomotive's fire, was emptied of ash and clinker at the end of a turn but then needed to be cleaned out properly before the engine's next turn of duty. At Neyland shed the job of 'box boy' was reserved for the newest recruit, and thus cleaner Bill Morgan was asked to tackle this task on his first morning there in 1916. Climbing into the firebox, he soon realised that, although the fire had

been removed, the confined space in which he was now crouching was still radiating a significant degree of heat! Using only a flare lamp for illumination, he was shown how to use a wire brush to scrape all the muck from the walls of the 'box and a primitive hook to remove clinker, which had been trapped in between the fire bars. Emerging from the cauldron covered from head to toe in ash and grime, he realised on sitting down to lunch that his cheese sandwich, which he had forgotten to remove from his pocket, had melted! He was starving, however, and enjoyed every bite![4]

Mention has already been made of the extremely high standard of cleanliness enjoyed by locomotives prior to World War 1. What is clear both from written reminiscences and oral testimony is that, as the years passed, these standards slipped, due in most part to shortages of labour and particularly the effects of war. Although the Locomotive Department was able eventually to recover from the labour shortages and difficulties caused by World War 1, matters became much worse when hostilities broke out again in

Right:
The cleaner's task (1):
a filthy Collett goods
locomotive awaits cleaning
at Swindon shed in the
1950s.

Below right:
The cleaner's task (2):
the untidy cab of an
unidentified GWR
locomotive, photographed by
Jim Russell in the 1940s.

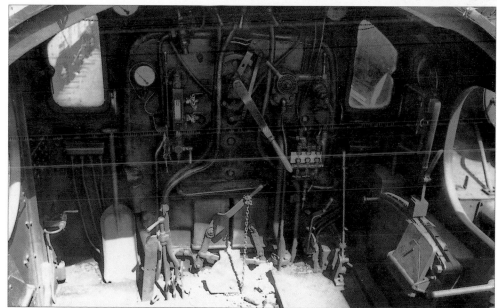

1939. As well as shortages of staff, the huge amount of work being undertaken at Swindon Works to produce munitions and other material for the war effort inevitably meant that prewar standards of maintenance and repair slipped. As a result, such cleaning as was done concentrated largely on the working parts of the locomotive, so that the driver preparing the engine could get around it without becoming too filthy and could see where lubrication was necessary. In his evocative account of life at Wolverhampton's Stafford Road shed, Geoff Brown, who began his career there in 1941, described the task of an engine-cleaner in those wartime years. The gang would tackle an engine, each scraping off what he called 'cheesy black muck', then wiping with cotton waste until, 'to the mild surprise of everyone, clean bright metal would often be revealed'. To enable cleaners to see when working under engines, they did not have the benefit of electric light, as would be expected today, but instead used flare lamps; Geoff Brown likened these to 'Aladdin's lamps', although there the comparison must end, as these paraffin lamps gave off a light of varying intensity according to how much of the wick protruded from its spout. They emitted acrid smoke as well as flame, adding to the already gloomy atmosphere in the shed.

As labour shortages intensified during the war years, made worse by increasing numbers of men being called up for military duty, standards decreased further. Matters were made worse by the fact that those same labour shortages meant that cleaners were promoted to junior firing turns much more quickly than they might have been in peacetime.

Above: The stores at Bristol Bath Road. It was here that both cleaners and footplate staff obtained supplies to carry out their work. The scales in the foreground were used to weigh out the cotton waste used by cleaners.

Below: The gloomy interior of Cardiff Canton shed in the early 1950s.
The picture was taken to illustrate an accident in the shed.

Above: The more modern surroundings of Radyr shed in South Wales after its rebuilding in 1931.
National Railway Museum

Below: A murky image of Landore shed in Swansea, with the coal stage on the left.
A GWR diesel railcar can be seen on the extreme right of the picture.

A postwar picture illustrating Tony Barfield's story about cleaning a locomotive thoroughly and revealing its original GWR livery. This engine has also had a crude 'BR' marked on its tanks.

Unlike in some other areas of the railway, the introduction of women to the Locomotive Department was not as rapid as it could have been, largely because of the entrenched attitude of senior staff. In 1941, for example, the Great Western Railway was employing only 45 female staff in locomotive sheds, as against 1,428 on the LMS. These figures were clearly an embarrassment to F. W. Hawksworth, the Chief Mechanical Engineer, who, writing to Divisional Superintendents in August 1942, noted: 'The poor results obtained up to now may be due to the fact that some foremen are prejudiced against the employment of female labour, but this prejudice must be broken down.'[5] Eventually more women were employed, although labour shortages continued both during and after the war.

It was clear that after the end of hostilities in 1945 it would take some time to return the locomotive fleet to prewar standards of cleanliness; some idea of just how dirty engines were can be gleaned from the story told by Tony Barfield, who, working at Kidderminster shed in the 1950s, described how he and his colleagues realised that a 2-6-2

The 'Boiler Gang' from the workshops at Ebbw Junction shed in 1924.

Hawksworth 'County' 4-6-0 No 1016 *County of Hants* in the engine shed at Swindon in July 1961.

tank locomotive (No 4153) stabled there had not been thoroughly cleaned for years. Removing layer upon layer of muck from the boiler and side tanks, they discovered that the engine was not actually black but green! Underneath all the grease and dirt the weathered paintwork still carried the magic initials of the Company, as did two other locomotives at the shed, which on further examination also proved to be still carrying their original Great Western livery.

In large sheds, there was always a variety of engines requiring cleaning. Gordon Shurmer remembers that the first tank locomotive he cleaned was 0-6-0 saddle tank No 2070, built at Swindon in 1899, while the first large passenger engine he tackled was 'Saint' 4-6-0 No 2947 *Madresfield Court*, built at the same works in 1912. Although he describes cleaning engine boilers, wheels and cab roofs, one place cleaners were not allowed at Swindon running shed was the locomotive cab. One day, while he was working on a '31xx' 2-6-2, one of his fellow cleaners pointed out a very unusual tank locomotive which had appeared in the shed. It was in all probability one of the small tank engines used in the South Wales docks, but its non-Swindon design and strange cab layout attracted the attention of the young cleaners, who clambered up into the cab for a closer look. Unfortunately for Gordon, as he pulled himself up into the cab he looked over to see the face of Mr Duck, the

Head Foreman, looking back at him from the other side of the engine. When he got down from the engine, as instructed, Gordon was shown the door by Mr Duck and told to go home for the day — a harsh punishment for what today seems a very minor misdemeanour.

Despite the strict discipline within locomotive sheds, the fact that large numbers of young men were working together led to all manner of pranks and tricks being played, both among the cleaners and on more senior members of staff. Almost every account written or told by a member of footplate staff is full of tales of scrapes with authority at one time or another during his time as a cleaner and afterwards. It was common for new or young cleaners to be shut into locomotive fireboxes or smokeboxes by their colleagues. It is not recorded that anyone was ever killed or seriously injured in such escapades, but spending half an hour in a hot, dusty and dark firebox cannot have been a pleasant experience! Tony Barfield recounted an occasion at Kidderminster shed when he was trapped in a firebox to 'sweat it out' whilst his colleagues took a tea break; unfortunately for him, as he became more panic-stricken and uncomfortable, his shouts for help were heard by the Shed Foreman, who was less than amused, and both victim and culprits were punished by being given the particularly filthy job of scraping the walls of the outside inspection pits.

While the punishment meted out to Gordon Shurmer for climbing into the cab of a locomotive may seem somewhat harsh today, the rule practised then was not without some reason. Given the number of locomotives stabled in such close proximity in a shed environment, the possibility of accidents and mishaps was high. As well as the day-to-day accidents of staff falling into pits or falling from locomotives whilst clambering over them, there was always the danger of cleaners or other shed staff being injured or killed by moving locomotives. Harold Gasson recounted the story of a driver who was killed when working under a locomotive at Didcot shed. Oiling his engine, he was crushed when another locomotive was roughly shunted into his, trapping him.

Prominent 'Not to be Moved' signs were fixed to locomotive lamp brackets when engines were being worked on, but this did not prevent serious accidents from occurring all the same. In a booklet issued by the Great Western Railway in January 1933 staff were warned: 'No one but a Driver, registered Fireman (or Shed Hand specially authorised to do so) is allowed to move an engine in steam . . . Engine Cleaners are not allowed to move any engine in steam under any circumstances whatever.'[6] Another area of concern to managers was one shared by their counterparts in the Goods Department: the booklet also reminded staff that 'under no circumstances must they pass between the buffers of Engines or other vehicles which are about to be brought together or are standing in close proximity'.[7]

Dangers were compounded at night, when the already Stygian gloom of the shed was magnified a thousandfold, and accidents were common, particularly during the wartime Blackout, when the level of lighting available to staff making their way around the shed was even more limited.

As the most junior members of staff, engine-cleaners were naturally expected to carry out the most menial and filthy jobs in the depot. These might include making up the fire in the foreman's office, helping out in the shed stores or assisting with all manner of other jobs. One task, which was always the province of the most junior staff, was that of 'call boy'. In every shed it was essential that footplate staff arrive on time for their turn, so early each morning (and sometimes at night) one of the young cleaners would tour the streets close to the depot, calling up locomotive crews for duty. This could be a difficult task, particularly if the person being summoned was a heavy sleeper. The problem was that in the early hours the call boy's attempts to waken his 'target' also tended to wake half the street, who took a dim view of the noise! In his affectionate reminiscences of life on the footplate Bill Morgan described his experiences waking

The crowded scene at Barry shed, with scores of 0-6-2T freight locomotives stabled awaiting duty.

bleary-eyed drivers at Neyland in South Wales, noting that some needed much persuasion to answer his knock while others needed 'only the slightest tap of the knuckles' on the door.[8]

The memories of Ron Smith give us a further example of the variety of tasks, other than engine-cleaning, undertaken by the most junior staff. Beginning his career at Southall, he was dismayed to discover that his first job would be that of cleaning the shed itself; this involved sweeping the floor between the tracks, shoving all the clinker, coal and dirt into the pits and then shovelling the waste into wheel-barrows. This was not only ex-hausting work for a 16-year-old but also left him with blisters all over his hands. Having dumped the waste at the tip, he and his mate were then expected to sort out all the waste coal they had collected, and return it to the coal stage!

As well as unloading wet sand from wagons, Ron spent much time working in the shed's lamp room, a corrugated-iron structure where firemen would collect the oil headlamps needed for their locomotive. Staff would return

A Great Western locomotive headlamp.

these when the locomotive returned to the shed; coming on duty at 10pm, Ron would be faced with the prospect of around 100 lamps to clean! The lamps themselves were heavy, and only four could be accommodated on the workbench at any one time. Once there they had their reservoirs removed, checked and filled with paraffin. The lamp lenses and reflector were then polished, the reservoir was replaced and the wick was checked to ensure it was in good condition.[9]

Although the cleaner's job was seen as the first foot on the ladder to life on the footplate, there were many other important if unglamorous jobs in the locomotive shed. It was reckoned that most Great Western locomotives worked for around 16 hours out of every 24, and, as well as the cleaners, firemen and drivers who lavished care on them, there were many others who helped keep them running. When an engine returned from its rostered duty, the fire was removed from the firebox; we have already mentioned the subsequent task of cleaning the inside of the 'box by junior staff, but the 'fire-dropper' had the even more onerous task

of shovelling out all the ash and clinker before this could be done. By the time the locomotive crew brought the engine back to the shed the fire had for the most part died down, so that it contained mostly ash, partly burnt coal and clinker. The last-named has been described by some firemen as having the consistency of volcanic lava, and it was seldom easy to shift. The fire-dropper had to remove all the ash and clinker through the small firebox door on the footplate, using specially manufactured clinker shovels, some measuring up to 14ft in length. Working from back to front, so as to avoid the shovel becoming red hot, the fire-dropper carefully removed the fire from fireboxes which might contain up to a ton of coal; the firebox on a 'King' measured 11ft 6in by 4ft. Once this was done he had to clamber under the loco-motive and empty its ashpan into the pit below. Not surprisingly these staff had a reputation for toughness — Gordon Shurmer recalls that their hands had the consistency of leather and that they could pick up hot coals with their bare hands!

Possibly the toughest staff in the shed were those who worked in the ashpits. Although on occasions the pits were damped down to reduce the effects of the dust, they were terrible places to work. Staff shovelling the ash out of the pit wore old sets of overalls, which they kept separately in their lockers. As Frank McKenna noted, they were never washed, as it would have been impossible to remove the oil, dust and perspiration with which they were caked; once they had become too soiled they would be burned in a locomotive firebox. For staff working in the ashpit, the outfit was completed by a pair of goggles, a handkerchief tied around the mouth and a pair of thick yellow boots. Thick-soled boots were needed as the ash and clinker that lay in the pit after being raked out from the locomotive firebox could be hot enough to burn the leather off an unsuspecting cleaner's boots! No wonder that ashpits were known as 'dust holes'.

Once shovelled out of the pit, the ash and clinker would have to be laboriously shovelled into railway wagons before being sent off shed. Much of the ash was dumped at places like Swindon Works, where it was used to build up the level of the land. Some still-warm clinker and ash was discovered

this operation only took place every few weeks; generally, with a warm engine, the whole process took more like a couple of hours.

A feature of most steam locomotive sheds was a sand furnace, employed to dry the sand used in the sandboxes fitted to all Great Western engines. Ron Smith, who worked at Southall shed in the 1950s, remembered as a young man being employed to stoke the two stationary boilers that dried the sand and powered the radiators and tube-blowing equipment. The fire holes for the two boilers were about 3ft above the ground level — an awkward height that added to his exhaustion and blisters from shovelling. He recalled that the job was particularly horrible, with all the ash blowing into his eyes; he also thought that these boilers needed stoking more than that of any main-line express locomotive!

Most sheds had a fitter to tackle any day-to-day maintenance that might be required on the locomotives stabled there. Not surprisingly, at larger sheds the workshop facilities were more elaborate, and at locations such as Old Oak Common fairly complex repairs could be carried out without the need for locomotives to be sent to Swindon Works. The late Tony Coles, who, having begun his career on British Railways' Western Region in 1952, spent his entire life as a railwayman, was apprenticed as a fitter at Taunton and Swindon, before moving to Old Oak in December 1957. (He was later to become Traction Maintenance Engineer there in the late 1960s and was heavily involved in the introduction of High Speed Trains on the Western Region.) In the steam era, throughout the early part of his career Tony kept a fascinating record of the work he did as a fitter, with a series of hand-written notebooks listing the engines he worked on, and the time spent on each job. A sample from one of these notebooks gives a good idea of the work the depots did to keep engines running; the book details repairs carried out on 'Kings' either based at Old Oak Common or which had been reported there with faults.

Locomotive No 6023 *King Edward II*, now being restored by the Great Western Society at Didcot, makes a number of appearances, the notebook recording several occasions when the engine was brought into the depot with hot bearings: in

during redevelopment of railway land at Swindon in the 1970s; the waste's high coal content led to its catching fire, leading to some hurried damping-down by contractors before it could be fully excavated!

The rostered turns worked by Great Western locomotives meant that, although they might well have had their fire dropped at the end of a duty, the water in the boiler was still warm a few hours later, when another vital member of the team — the 'lighter-up' — began the process again by preparing the locomotive for its duty the next day. Small but cleverly thought-out wooden cubes of timber, usually consisting of up to 11 pieces of scrap timber, were used to start the fire, along with the ubiquitous cotton waste found all over the depot. Another member of staff, sometimes known as the 'steam-raiser', was then deputed to ensure that the fire was built up and maintained, so that when the footplate crew arrived, around an hour and a half before the rostered duty, there was enough pressure in the boiler to raise steam. From cold, after a boiler wash-out, it might take seven or eight hours to get up to working pressure, although

A photograph taken by a member of the CME's department to illustrate the introduction of a special elevated skip system to aid coaling of engines. Whether the scheme was adopted is not recorded.

July 1952 this was on the leading bogie; three years later, on 1 September 1955, the locomotive's leading left-hand axlebox had run hot and the 'engine was sent to us'. On the latter occasion the oil pads were cleaned out, new horsehair was put in, and the locomotive was sent on to Laira shed the same day! Two further pages of Tony Coles' log note that on 20 September 1956 the engine had hit a lorry at Bruton in Somerset; details of the accident itself are not recorded, but the Old Oak fitters were called to Platform 5 at Paddington in order to examine the engine, which had suffered 'bad damage to bogie and inside cylinder cock gear'.[10] The locomotive was 'stopped' (taken out of service) and presumably towed back to the depot. Strangely, however, repair work did not begin until almost a week later, Tony's log recording that the front bogie was so badly damaged that it had to be returned to Swindon for repairs. In the interim a replacement was sent to Old Oak and fitted to the engine. Various pipes and rods were straightened, and, while the engine was out of service, the opportunity was also taken to check the water-gauge frame and to renew the gauge glass itself. Finally, the log notes, the engine brakes were 'adjusted', with all work being completed by 2 November 1956.

Not all sheds had anywhere near the facilities provided at Old Oak Common; after all, in 1947, this was home to 232 locomotives, from the mighty 'Kings' to lowly 0-6-0 pannier tanks. However, as well as a coal stage, most reasonably sized sheds would have sand furnaces, a boiler house, offices and stores. The design of sheds varied dramatically; some dated back to the Victorian period, although many had been replaced or upgraded early in the 20th century, when G. J. Churchward became Locomotive Superintendent. Further improvements were made in the 1930s, when Government money, made available to alleviate the crippling effects of unemployment, was used by the Great Western to upgrade some of its facilities.

It seems, however, that the age and design of sheds did not always make a huge impact on the conditions endured by the staff. The very nature of steam locomotives and the large amounts of soot, ash and clinker generated by their operation did not engender cleanliness, however fine the facilities were! Geoff Brown described Stafford Road shed on his first morning. 'Can you imagine the scene? The great shed with its two massive turntables, and all around the ghostly shapes of locomotives, all of them patchily lit by the lofty gas lights.' Three engines awaited their next turn,

'surrounded by noise and activity, the bright light from the cabs and the steam rising from the damped-down coal indicating that they were almost ready for duty'.[11]

Facilities for shed staff were at best basic and were quite often graded in order of importance. Bernard Barlow described the arrangements at Didcot shed, where the offices of the shedmaster and running foreman were superior to the drivers' mess room, followed by those of the mechanical fitters, boilersmith fitters' mates, chargeman cleaners, shed staff and engine cleaners. These 'grade' distinctions were mirrored all over the system and in every department, even down to the toilets, where at most depots the supervisors had their own cubicle accessible by a key available only to them.[12] The camaraderie of the facilities, however dirty or primitive, is still remembered with affection by many retired railwaymen; indeed, although beginning as a cleaner and progressing through the grades to become a top-link driver might today seem an excessively long journey, few Western staff regretted their 'steam apprenticeship'.

4

On the Footplate

For junior staff, having experienced what might be politely described as a baptism of fire as an engine-cleaner, the next logical step was that of becoming a passed cleaner. Throughout their time as cleaners, they had an ideal opportunity not only to see Great Western steam locomotives at close quarters but also to pick up information and practical knowledge from more senior staff at the shed. There seems over the years to have been no set Company procedure for the employment of firemen from the ranks of cleaning staff and certainly each railwayman seems to have different memories of the way in which he finally became a fireman proper.

In the two years he had been a cleaner at Swindon running shed, Gordon Shurmer gradually gained experience and eventually, in 1939, was asked to be part of the 'spare' firing turn, deputising on occasions when needed; he was then made a 'temporary' fireman, again to be called on when sickness or staff shortages dictated. For this duty he was paid 9s 6d (47½p) per day, as opposed to the 4s (20p) per day he had received as an engine cleaner. With the outbreak of the World War 2 in the autumn of 1939 he was finally asked to report once again to Park House in Swindon for a medical to confirm his appointment as a permanent fireman.

Harold Gasson's first experience of firing a Great Western engine came one winter's morning in February 1941, when, like Gordon Shurmer, he was asked to deputise for a sick member of staff who had failed to turn up for work. Glad to be escaping the confined spaces of a 'Hall' firebox, he left the

The driver on the footplate of a 'Castle', oiling various fittings on the boiler backplate.

A posed Company photograph of a 'King', No 6026 *King John*, seen with its crew in 1936.

shed and booked on at Didcot West 'box. The West End pilot link was a shunting turn, and the locomotive onto which he climbed was an ancient 0-6-0 tank engine (No 907) built in 1875. This antique still had an open cab, but, as Gasson relates, at that moment it could have been *King George V* for all he cared. As was often the case, the locomotive driver was one of the more senior members of the complement at the shed, who, although careful to let the young cleaner know who was boss, was nevertheless prepared to show him the ropes, in more ways than one! The absent fireman remained off sick for a week, so Harold was able to complete a whole week's worth of firing duties. From then on, opportunities to take the shovel became more frequent, on yard pilot duties and in the Royal Ordnance Depot at Didcot, which was producing large amounts of material for the war effort.

Within months, no doubt accelerated by the pressure of the war and the shortage of trained footplate staff, Harold was asked to take on a far bigger firing job, on the 7.37am Didcot–Southampton service. Fortunately he was working with an experienced and sympathetic driver, and a well-maintained 'Bulldog' locomotive, No 3376 *River Plym*. He acquitted himself well but after a week was back down to earth with a bump, returning to the grime of the depot. It was not until his 17th birthday later in the year that he finally received the letter he had been hoping for, confirming that he was at last registered as a Great Western fireman.

Harold Gasson's letter from Swindon had not only confirmed his status as a fireman but had also given him a registered number for seniority. This concept dominated the life of footplate staff, even in the darkest days of the war, when the seemingly inexorable time it took to rise up the ranks had been speeded up. Once staff were on the footplate they could move up the ladder only by progressing through the links, starting at the bottom on relief duties, before moving on to shunting or yard work, then branch or local trains or goods services, before finally reaching the top passenger links. This process was repeated for drivers, although firemen would not necessarily continue naturally through the links to become a driver. An example of the range of links at a shed can be gleaned from the following list, which outlines the arrangements at Banbury shed just after World War 2, when it had over 120 crews and around 80 locomotives.[1] The work was dominated by goods traffic, although in the 1940s the locomotive allocation comprised a wide variety of mixed-traffic locomotives, including 'Hall', 'Grange' and 'Manor' 4-6-0s, as well as over two dozen '28xx' heavy-freight 2-8-0s.

No 1 Link

Passenger duties, Didcot and Leamington; passenger shunting (12 turns)

No 2 Link

Auto duties, Kingham & Wycombe (four turns) (Prewar this link had a Senior Driver/Junior Fireman progression but returned to natural progression after 1945)

No 3 Link

'Top Goods' — vacuum goods trains, excursion and special passenger duties; through goods, Old Oak Common (12 turns)

No 4 Link

Express goods, Old Oak Common, Reading, Bordesley (12 turns)

Nos 5 and 6 Links

Goods, ironstone to Cardiff, Brill, Bletchington, Old Oak Common; local goods (12 turns per link)

No 7 Link

Goods and relief, Bristol goods to Didcot, relieving crews of goods trains *en route* (six turns from shed, six relief)

Nos 8 and 9 Links

Goods and relief, zone relief; used for specials, replacing sick crew, engine preparation, shed work. (No 8 Link: two turns and 10 relief duties)

No 10 Link

Pilot duties in yards (progressive link)

No 11 Link

Pilot duties in yards (non-progressive link)

As staff progressed up through the links, they left vacancies, so more junior staff were able to fill their places; progression was also aided by natural wastage within the ranks. There was no way to buck the system, however, and staff had patiently to wait their turn, until a position became vacant. Matters were slightly easier if staff were prepared to move to another depot, but for more senior staff, married with families, this was not so easy. For the younger footplatemen, with few ties, the ability to move could speed up the process somewhat.

Having begun his career as an engine-cleaner at Hereford, Tom Conduit moved to Whitland in West Wales and there gained further experience taking instructions from footplate staff while still working on the more day-to-day tasks he was required to perform as a cleaner. He remembers helping with lighting-up, which gave him more experience and familiarity with the management of the fire, and did his first stint on the shovel on a trip to Pembroke Dock in 1941, filling in for a fireman who had failed to turn up for work; he had had no formal training but relied on the instructions given to him by the driver.

In 1942, when he turned 17, Tom passed out as a fireman and moved to St Philip's Marsh shed in Bristol, where he found himself working with more than 30 other young firemen. He recalls that his first priority was to find lodgings, which he duly did in nearby Totterdown, for the princely sum of 25s per week. Again, seniority came into play, and Tom found himself in the 'Engine Control' link, which involved taking locomotives 'light' (single) to places where they were required. From this he went on to shunting duties at Stoke Gifford yard (the site of today's Bristol Parkway station). This task, working with driver Vic Farr, proved good practice for the new fireman, for Vic allowed him to take the regulator for much of the time. The work involved shunting rakes of coal and mineral wagons, and during this spell Tom experienced his first 'breakaway' (the snapping of a wagon coupling). The advice of his more senior colleague was that he should allow more time to 'stretch' the train's couplings before fully opening the regulator — a process he should reverse when braking. At this time staff worked a six-day, 48-hour week; for footplate crews (unlike the staff at Swindon Works) Saturday was a normal working day. Younger staff like Tom would often seize the opportunity to earn extra money by working on Sundays, especially during the war years, when shortages of staff meant that there was always work available for those wanting it. At this time firemen earned around £3 per week, giving considerable spending power to those who, like Tom, were in lodgings.

Tom next had a spell in the 'Transfer Link', working in virtually all the goods yards in the Bristol area, including both the City and Avonmouth docks. At the top of this particular link seniority once again came into play, and he then began at the bottom of the next rung in the ladder, working at Bristol Bath Road engine shed, preparing locomotives for the road. The task of getting large locomotives like 'Castles' and 'Kings' ready for their crews

A 1938 view of a driver using his feeder-oil can to lubricate the motion of a 'Star' locomotive.

was hard, dirty work and involved making up the fire and building up steam from around 30-40lb to a full working pressure of 180lb. Each class of locomotive was allotted a particular length of time for its preparation; the largest passenger types needed 70 minutes, whilst tank engines required less than an hour. As well as preparing the fire, he broke up coal in the tender, checked the smokebox and cleaned the footplate as best he could; the driver then arrived to oil the locomotive ready for departure.

Since his family were still in West Wales, Tom applied to return there and finally obtained employment as a fireman at Carmarthen. From there he fired on trains all around West Wales, working on passenger and goods services on the Aberystwyth line as well as to Fishguard, Neyland and Milford Haven. The largely rural nature of this part of Wales must have provided a stark contrast to Bristol, where, as well as experiencing life as a new fireman, he had had to contend with the dangers of the Blitz, which had been particularly bad in the city.

Most accounts of the transition from cleaner to fireman in the late 1930s and 1940s involve the new recruit's filling in for absent or sick staff as a valuable means of gaining experience. However, in the years before, particularly during the Great Depression, competition for firing jobs was much tougher, especially as the Company had a rule that the minimum age for promotion from cleaner to fireman was 25. The downturn in business caused by the General Strike and the Wall Street Crash meant that, with fewer trains being run, fewer footplate staff were needed, and, consequently, promotion was non-existent. The age limit was dispensed with, and without promotions and retirements there was no chance for those lower down the links to move up; indeed, as the number of cleaners grew, there were rumours that some might have to be laid off. With almost three million unemployed, this was not a prospect that many viewed with enthusiasm.

In his account of his career, Alf Summers recorded that it took him more than 10 years to progress from cleaner to fireman at Old Oak Common. In his book *Engines Good and Bad* he notes that during the 1920s he had managed just two footplate trips, one on a '2301' 'Dean Goods' and the other, more significantly, on one of the most famous Great Western engines, *The Great Bear* — the Company's sole Pacific. It was not until the summer of 1933 that he finally got his chance to take on a firing duty. With such a long 'apprenticeship', it was not surprising that he thought that the driver he accompanied on a shunting turn 'had little to tell me'.[2] Despite a number of similar outings, he was not made up to a fireman until December 1934.

Gordon Shurmer also described his time on the footplate as an 'apprenticeship'. Having passed his medical in October 1939 he too began his firing career working on shunting turns, graduating to more substantial work on freight trains to more distant locations. By 1947 he had reached the Top Link as a fireman, working with driver Bill Hinder on express passenger services from Swindon to destinations

An Edwardian image of the footplate team. The fireman has a hefty load of coal on his shovel!

such as Cardiff and Leicester, the latter a regular turn for Swindon crews. At the peak of his career as fireman, Gordon worked with Bill for almost seven years and during this time learned a great deal; his driver was someone who 'liked things right' but helped to pass on knowledge to his young assistant. Unusually, Gordon was able to stay at Swindon shed for the whole of his career and, unlike so many drivers and firemen during their working lives, did not need to move away to gain promotion.

At this point it would be useful to give a brief description of what a fireman's duties might entail on a typical working day. Arriving on shed, the fireman would book on at the Time Office; exactly when a fireman booked on would depend on the size of locomotive and the turn rostered; as we have already discovered from the recollections of Tom Conduit, who prepared engines during World War 2, the time needed might vary from 45 minutes to well over an hour.

The fireman would collect from the stores the appropriate small tools and keys to the locomotive toolboxes. He would also make sure that the engine had a complete set of lamps, including the locomotive headlamps, a water-gauge-glass lamp and a flare lamp, topping up the reservoirs of the headlamps and trimming and cleaning them ready for use. The rules and regulations required that the locomotive should carry two red flags and no fewer than 12 detonators for emergency use, so these too needed to be checked and replenished if necessary.

Climbing up into the cab, the fireman knew that, unless there had been problems on shed beforehand, the locomotive should already have more than enough water in the boiler, a reasonable fire in the firebox and a boiler pressure that was steady, albeit below that necessary for the engine to leave the shed. In the booklet 'Fuel Efficiency on the Footplate', issued by the Great Western Railway in 1945, it was noted that the fireman's first task was to check the water gauge. This was situated on the boiler backplate and indicated to the crew the amount of water contained in the boiler. Clearly, if this gauge were not working properly, the consequences would be extremely serious, both to the locomotive's boiler and to the safety of the crew, so it was imperative that it be checked.

Beneath the metal protector was the gauge glass, which although made of extremely tough glass, could break. Harold Gasson described how a driver he worked with as a young man had deliberately broken the glass, filling the cab with hot steam and water, vividly illustrating the dangers of steam locomotives. Already familiar with the layout of the cab and its fittings, Harold was able to reach through the steam and turn the water gauge handle to the 'off' position, but it was a valuable lesson, and from that point on, like most drivers and fireman, he always carried a couple of spare glasses and the rubber washers needed to fit them.

The next task was to prepare the fire and start to build it up; to do this the fire was spread evenly over the entire grate, with a few shovelfuls of 'lump' coal sprinkled over it to start it

burning more rapidly. The dampers could then be opened and the blower applied to increase combustion. The fireman then continued firing at intervals, with each successive load of coal added creating a bed of coal 'suitable for the class of train to be worked'.[3] Once this had been done, he would check the rest of the locomotive, beginning by ensuring that the sandboxes were full. The smokebox door was then opened and the tube plates checked; once the door had been securely closed and tightened, the fireman would brush away any ashes that had been displaced from inside from the footplate, as any ash or debris would not only look unsightly but might also get inside the locomotive's motion. By this time the driver had usually arrived, having (after booking on) collected enough oil from the stores to lubricate the locomotive.

The job of preparing an engine was very much a 'team effort', reflecting the whole ethos of good engine management. While the driver made his way around the locomotive, oiling the scores of reservoirs, oil boxes and surfaces which required lubrication, the fireman would continue building up the fire and would check that both the injectors were working. He would also climb up into the tender and break up and stack the coal, ensuring that it was of a manageable size for the journey. Once this was done he would hose down the footplate area, usually with water from the coal-watering pipe. Even when materials and tools were short, the discipline of ensuring a clean and tidy cab was always maintained.

Tools were another item to be checked. Ensuring that an engine had its full complement of equipment was extremely important — even more so during the war years, when some tools and equipment were in short supply. Tom Conduit remembered that some tools were so scarce that a fireman, walking around the depot and seeing something he needed

Right:
Preparations for the journey complete, the crew of 'Saint' No 2950 *Taplow Court* wait on the platform at Paddington

Below:
Driver Clem Ricks from Swindon shed on the footplate of an unidentified 'King' 4-6-0.
STEAM / Kenneth Leech collection

for his turn, would often remove that item from another engine and hide it until required. Matters deteriorated to the point that the Company proposed an 'amnesty' for tools which had been hidden in staff lockers and other parts of the locomotive shed!

Needless to say, the fireman's most important tool was his shovel. E. H. Terry, who had begun his career on the Great Western in 1919, described the ideal shovel as being about 20in long and about 9in wide, with the ends cut back slightly to make it easier for transferring coal from tender to firebox. Many top-link firemen had their own shovels, modified by shed fitters, often with the handle shortened or lengthened to suit their height and reach. Terry confessed to keeping two shovels with him on the locomotive after the embarrassment of putting both coal and firing shovel into the firebox on one occasion during the early part of his career![4]

Almost all footplate staff to whom the author has spoken have mentioned the firing shovel's other use, which has become part of railway folklore — its impromptu transformation into a frying pan! At quiet times, particularly on a shunting turn, bacon and eggs could be cooked for a hungry crew. E. H. Terry also noted that at the end of a

Driver Ernie Sims of Swindon shed.
STEAM / Kenneth Leech collection

journey, with a large lump of coal at one end, the shovel could hold just enough hot water to provide a decent wash, the water being supplied from the coal watering pipe described earlier. Some staff also mentioned a later 'killjoy' who specified that shovels should have holes drilled in them to prevent any misuse, culinary or otherwise, by staff.

Another piece of equipment usually carried by footplate staff was the 'Grimsby' box, named after the town where these large steel boxes were manufactured. Made specifically for enginemen, they usually contained sandwiches and cold tea, the latter in an old whisky bottle; it was not until World War 2 that the tea cans were introduced that would become so common in British Rail days. Enginemen were issued with supplies of tea, sugar and condensed milk to help them cope with some of the long shifts they endured during the war years, and the tea cans, manufactured by boilersmiths at Old Oak Common, became standard issue. In later years imported enamel tins were also used, both types being held in the firebox on the end of the shovel; in the searing heat of the 'box the water boiled within seconds, and the resultant brew was described by Bernard Barlow as 'a sort of alcoholic tea', the taste of which, even long after retirement, he still remembered with affection.

As well as containing sustenance for the journey, the Grimsby box was often used by footplate staff to store spare detonators, flags and water gauge glasses. Opening the flap inside the lid, one might also find a copy of the Company Rules & Regulations and one or two books on railway operation, such as A. F. Hunt's *Descriptive Diagrams of the Locomotive*, that could be perused in spare moments. This booklet was produced through the efforts of the 'Mutual Improvement Classes' at both Oxford and Oswestry depots, Mr Hunt, a driver at Oswestry, being also an instructor at these voluntary classes; in the preface to the booklet he remarks: 'It is difficult to show others at times, even if one knows oneself; imparting that knowledge to others is a far different matter . . . I would also like to say how well the M.I.C. is progressing, and we are proud of the brotherly feeling that exists.'[5] The classes were a good place for up-and-coming footplate staff to learn more about the mysteries and working of the steam locomotive and were augmented by various publications issued both by the Company and, particularly, by staff such as A. F. Hunt. Another example of this self-help was a publication, *Questions & Answers on the Walschaerts Valve Gear*, written by M. J. Kimber, an instructor at the Swindon Mutual Improvement Class. This booklet, profits from which were in aid of the MIC, was issued as a response to the newer British Railways Standard locomotives being introduced on to the Western Region in the 1950s. The author noted that the booklet had been 'expressly produced for footplate men, especially the younger men of the fraternity who will one day be in charge of these locomotives and require information on the subject; it may also be of assistance to firemen when preparing to pass the technical examination for promotion'.[6]

Claude Gardner and his unidentified colleague on the footplate of No 4079 *Pendennis Castle*, now in the care of the Great Western Society at Didcot. *STEAM / Kenneth Leech collection*

Returning to our reconstruction of a fireman's duties, the mention of washing brings us to almost the end of the preparation of the engine for the road. The footplate having been cleaned, it was time to take the locomotive to the shed's water column, to ensure that it had enough water for the journey. A number of reminiscences also mention the fact that many drivers actually changed into a cleaner and tidier set of overalls before leaving the shed, since crawling around under the engine during its oiling-up was a particularly dirty process.

Once on the road the junior fireman would find things very different and would need to remember all he had learned during his apprenticeship in the links. As Ted Abear, who worked his way through the links at Southall shed in the years after World War 2, noted, 'Firing in a yard and keeping an engine quiet was one thing; firing an engine on the main line and keeping a head of steam was another.' Fortunately, at Southall the 'lower links contained just about enough work on the main line to allow the aspiring Top Link fireman to aim for greater things'.[7]

The day-to-day reality of working as a fireman did illustrate the need for teamwork. In 'Fuel Efficiency on the Footplate', the Company described the duties of the fireman as being to 'regulate the fire and height of water according to the work to be performed, and to have full boiler pressure when it is required'; the latter should be achieved, however, without the safety valves' lifting on the boiler, since 'blowing off from the safety valves causes a serious waste of fuel' which was seen as a 'sign of bad judgement'. In short, the fireman was there to ensure the driver had a good supply

The fireman's view: approaching Reading station from the cab of the 'Castle' locomotive heading the 1.15pm Paddington–Bristol service in the 1950s.

of steam to allow him to run the locomotive; the driver had then to operate the engine in the most efficient and economic way possible. Gordon Shurmer summed up the aims of both footplatemen as being 'efficiency, punctuality and a safe journey', with the latter being the most important.

For the fireman the most difficult and taxing part of the job was, of course, keeping the firebox full of coal. The sheer effort of shovelling up to four tons of coal on a journey from Bristol to Paddington was exhausting, and it goes without saying that only the fittest firemen would last the pace. Quite apart from the exertions of shovelling, the fireman had to learn to lift the coal cleanly from the tender into the fire hole, without scattering a shovelful of coal across the cab floor — something not appreciated by the driver. Most firemen stuck to the axiom of 'little and often', firing to keep the grate well covered; having built up the corners and sides of the firebox, the fireman would then add coal to the middle, working hard to keep the balance of just enough coal to maintain pressure without the safety valves' lifting.

Being in charge of a 100-ton steam locomotive and its train, racing along the main line at 80mph, was without doubt a huge responsibility but one which was always taken seriously by both footplate staff and management. Both driver and fireman were responsible for the safety of their passengers, for, although it was the driver's job to watch for signals, the layout of Great Western locomotive cabs made this more difficult. This was because, unlike those of most British railway companies, the GWR's locomotives were driven from the right-hand side, while most (although not all) signals were situated on the left-hand side of the track! When not firing the fireman could play a vital role in sighting signals, although the ultimate responsibility still rested with the driver, who had to learn the route and ultimately sign to confirm that he 'knew the road'. The latter was the culmination of a long process of building up knowledge of all the signals, junctions and other features on a particular route or line. A GWR circular issued in 1947 by the Chief Mechanical Engineer's Department noted that a 'Knowledge of Roads' book was to be kept at each shed, 'containing particulars of the roads with which each Driver is acquainted and capable of working over'.[8] Drivers were required to sign for each individual route over which they were confident of working — a procedure that had to be repeated every six months. Each driver, the circular warned, 'is responsible for knowing the road over which he is booked to work, and if at all in doubt, must inform the foreman at once'.[9] Without such knowledge, it would be necessary for the crew to have on the footplate a 'pilotman' — a driver who was familiar with the route. Learning the road might also require footplate staff to ride along with another crew to gain experience of a particular route or service.

When booking on, the driver was responsible for checking any notices of speed restrictions or alterations to signals or services that had been issued by the Traffic Department. There was normally a weekly booklet noting such alterations, as well as a 'Late Notice' board on the wall, which alerted staff to any emergency changes to signalling or permanent-way work. Failing to pay heed to such changes could have potentially serious consequences; in his book *Didcot Engineman* Bernard Barlow records that the tragic accident which occurred on 20 November 1955 at Milton (near Didcot) was in some part due to the fact that the driver had not noted in the weekly notices issued to him that the up main line was being re-laid on that day, and that his train, had been diverted onto the up goods line. As a result, the locomotive, BR Standard Pacific No 70026 *Polar Star*, travelling at 50-60mph, plunged down a 20ft embankment after passing over a crossover normally traversed at 10mph. There were, of course, other factors contributing to the accident, which cost 11 lives and injured many more, including faulty ATC equipment and the absence of a hand signalman at the spot, but it clearly illustrates the fact that, at all times, footplate staff needed to know the route and any changes to it.[10]

The whole concept of route knowledge was not merely the ability to remember where signals were but extended much further than that: in the dark, wartime Blackout or (that bane of footplate crews) fog, older and more experienced drivers were able to identify their position on a line by senses other than just sight. Many could work out their position by sound — the sound of an engine as it passed through a cutting or across an embankment or under a bridge became, through experience, particularly recognisable. Drivers could also navigate by a sense of smell, the likes of a chocolate factory, a brewery or a creosote factory providing valuable indication as to location.

Gordon Shurmer remembers being helped by a driver who prevented him from using one of the long firing tools on a night-time trip. To use this awkward tool he would have had to lift it vertically above the height of the cab — a dangerous manœuvre on a stretch of line with numerous overbridges; had the 11ft poker hit one of the bridges, he could easily have been killed, but the driver's years of experience stopped the young fireman from putting himself in that perilous position.

Just how lucky Gordon was is apparent from the report of an accident that occurred in August 1931 involving the crew of 'Saint' locomotive No 2905 *Lady Macbeth* , hauling the 1am Paddington–Swansea service. As the train passed through Moreton Cutting, near Didcot, at about 60mph, Fireman Morris of Landore shed was killed when one of the large fire irons he was using struck an overbridge, throwing him off the engine. In reaching a verdict of Accidental Death, the Abingdon Coroner heard evidence that on newer locomotives (such as a 'King') a recess was provided by the side of the firebox, obviating the need to swing large fire irons to and fro from the side of the tender. The driver, Joe Thomas, who had been on the footplate for almost 36 years, reported that approaching the cutting he had been looking out of the right-hand window but, hearing a clatter, turned to see his mate disappear over the side of the footplate. The 38-year-old fireman left a wife and two children, who received £571 compensation from the Company.[11]

As well as a lump sum, the unfortunate widow of Fireman Morris would probably have received a pension from the Great Western Engine & Fireman's Mutual Assurance Sick & Superannuation Society, known to the men as the MAS. Although footplate crew had created their own fund for providing widow's benefits as early as 1856, it was not until 1865 that a Friendly Society was set up for 'the purpose of providing Assurance, Sick Benefits, Widows Allowance and Superannuation'.[12] In due course, membership of this scheme became compulsory, and the author of the Society's history, published on its centenary in 1965, considered that by doing this in those early days the Great Western Railway hoped that membership would invalidate any claim by staff and would also engender loyalty, since anyone leaving the railway's employment would lose any benefits they might have accrued. By the 1930s subscription rates varied from 2s 4d to 3s 10d for 'First-class' members and from 1s 8d to

The aftermath of the accident at Milton in November 1955, before the locomotive was righted and lifted clear of the scene.

The driver's view: his 'Castle' 4-6-0 is overtaking a slow goods hauled by a '28xx' 2-8-0
on the quadrupled stretch of line between Paddington and Reading.

3s 9d for 'Second-class' members. Sick pay was 14s and 12s respectively for the first 26 weeks, reducing by about a third after this date. Pensions were paid at 60 years of age or upon disablement, at 5s and 3s 6d respectively, in addition to a lump sum granted by the fund. Widows could also receive a pension up to a maximum of between 3s and 6s per week, according to length of service, and, if there was no widow, dependent children also received an allowance.

Compared with other main-line railways, the Great Western (and its successor, British Railways Western Region) suffered few serious accidents. All the same, the crashes at Shrivenham in 1932 and Norton Fitzwarren in 1942 proved that the footplate could be a dangerous place to work. Great Western footplate crews were, however, fortunate in having a back-up system to help ensure the safety of their passengers and train. Automatic Train Control (ATC) was a Company invention, first tested on the railway in 1906 on the Henley branch line but eventually installed almost all over the

system. Ramps laid between the rails were linked to signals, so that, as the train approached a distant signal which was at Caution, when the locomotive passed over the ramp a siren would sound in the cab, warning the driver that the following home signal might well be at Danger; the driver could then cancel the warning by operating a lever on the ATC equipment on the footplate, failure to do so resulting in an automatic application of the train brakes. If the distant signal were showing Clear, as the locomotive passed over the ramp a bell would ring on the footplate, indicating 'all clear'. As most drivers would confirm, however, the ATC system was not an end in itself; it was there to assist drivers, since they always had to be vigilant, for despite the fact that a signal might indicate that the line was 'clear' there could be an obstruction on the line ahead.

As noted earlier, the ultimate aim of most firemen was to become a driver. Having gained experience on a variety of links, they would eventually be summoned to Swindon

The view from the open cab of this GWR 0-6-0 pannier tank would have been good but cold when running cab-first, as seen in this picture, and uncomfortable in wet weather!

for another medical and 'Examination for Promotion'. Alf Summers, whose early career as an engine-cleaner was described in the previous chapter, received the call to return to Park House on 5 June 1944 — more than 21 years after he had begun service with the Company. He remarked that the years of experience and the tuition he had received at the Didcot depot's Mutual Improvement Class stood him in good stead, and he was able to answer the questions posed by the Inspector. As most drivers would agree, all the hours spent on the footplate counted for much, but on the day that they stepped onto the locomotive for the first time as its driver the feeling was quite different. Alf noted that, although he had probably worked over 300 jobs as a fireman, 'I had put down the fireman's shovel and had taken on a vastly more responsible role'.[13]

Another Didcot man, Bernard Barlow, describing his feelings at achieving his boyhood ambition, wrote that, arriving at Paddington to take the train, 'I had a sudden light-headed feeling. For years I had groomed myself for this moment, and I was not going to allow anything to upset my great joy.'[14] At Old Oak Common shed his euphoria increased when he and his mate were asked to take out 'Castle' No 5029 *Nunney Castle* on a return excursion, in

place of the more lowly freight engine for which they had originally been booked. Not surprisingly, he and his fireman were keen to prove themselves to their colleagues by taking on this prestigious locomotive, but all was not what it seemed: they soon found out, as they guided their train out of Paddington and through West London, that, despite being one of the most powerful passenger types used on the Western, *Nunney Castle* was not performing well. As they discovered later, the engine was long overdue a boiler washout and was not really in any state to be used; despite all their efforts, it proved almost impossible to maintain boiler pressure, and the fire was lifeless. Struggling to maintain enough steam to operate the brakes, they were forced to pause at Slough for a 25min 'blow up'. This meant halting the train to allow the fire to be improved and boiler pressure built up. To locomotive men it was the ultimate humiliation, and when the dejected crew limped into Reading the engine was replaced with another 'Castle', No 5026, the station pilot. This was in far better condition, and the rest of the trip presented no problem. Bernard noted that, having been brought heavily down to earth on his first trip in charge, he gained what he called a 'nose' — the ability to 'smell' a bad engine. Discovering after the event that another crew,

A view of a train nearing Teignmouth in Devon as a 'County' class locomotive approaches heading a westbound service.

having seen the condition of *Nunney Castle*, had refused to take her out, he realised all too late that he and his colleague had been duped!

Tom Conduit became a driver in 1956, having in the interim served as a fireman at Swindon, where he moved in the summer of 1945. There he had once again worked his way up through the links, finally reaching the No 1 Passenger Link. Although this was the top link, he remembered it as being a difficult one to work, for, although it involved working passenger trains to destinations such as Paddington, Cardiff and Weston-super-Mare, three of its 12 turns involved a 2am start, and there were a number of other night workings.

Presented with the opportunity to become a driver, Tom applied to move to Old Oak Common. By this time he was married with a child, so his family moved to Hayes in West London, a few miles from the depot. Once again, seniority meant that he started on shunting links. After three years or

so he applied to return to Swindon. In due course a vacancy arose, and he was able to move back, to the relief of his family, who had not found the London smogs good for their health. Vacancies had arisen at Swindon because a number of younger drivers had left the railway entirely to work in the town's new Pressed Steel car plant, no doubt attracted by the more regular hours, better pay and cleaner working conditions. Tom started in what he described as the 'old men's link', working the branches to Malmesbury and Highworth and the old Midland & South Western Junction Railway route via Marlborough and Andover; eventually he moved up to the Control Link and thereafter stayed at Swindon until he retired.

Whilst most drivers toiled away on the day-to-day business of looking after the 'bread and butter' runs — the stopping passenger, goods and shunting turns — those employed in the top links at the largest depots (like Old Oak Common) were seen by the Company and the media as the

Under inspection. The crew of this 'Castle' have the beady eye of the Inspector on them, suggesting the locomotive is working a special test train from Swindon Works, in 1947.

élite. Writing in the *Great Western Railway Magazine* in July 1937, Driver Parsons of Old Oak Common described something of his job as one of the 24 most experienced men at the depot. By this time he had been a driver for 34 years, so (as already noted) the rise through the ranks was a slow one; indeed, at the time the article was published, he had less than three months to go before retirement.

The article was one of a series entitled 'Spotlight on My Job', and in it Driver Parsons outlined a typical day as the driver of Great Western's premier express service, the 'Cornish Riviera Limited'.[15] In illustrating the work of a driver and the relationship with his fireman one can do no better than to quote from and enlarge upon this account of his day's work nearly 70 years ago. The actual business of booking-on and engine preparation has been described earlier in the chapter, and our story continues from the point at which the engine left the depot, ready for work. As Old Oak Common depot was some miles from Paddington, the locomotive would be backed down over the main line at Kensal Green through what one writer has described as the 'brick canyon' to Royal Oak, where it would pause until given the road to back onto the express it would be hauling. The empty carriage stock would already have been shunted into position by one of the various pannier-tank locomotives employed for the purpose — a firing and driving turn the man in charge of the express locomotive might well have been employed on years before! As the main-line locomotive backed carefully towards the train, the fireman would jump down onto the ballast between the tracks and signal to the driver as he allowed the buffers of the tender to nudge into those of the leading carriage, hopefully without too much of a jolt. The driver keeping the hand brake screwed on, the fireman would then duck under the buffers and lift the heavy screw

coupling over the drawhook of the carriage. The vacuum-brake hoses would then be coupled up and checked. With very little room to manoeuvre, the fireman had a difficult and potentially dangerous task and one which had to be carried out with some care. Usually the driver would check the coupling himself before ensuring that the vacuum brakes were functioning correctly — something that was also checked by the passenger guard from the rear of the train.

The guard, having walked the length of the train at least twice to check the vacuum-brake hoses and connections on each vehicle, would then come to the locomotive and record the names of the crew, before notifying them of the weight

Driver Cottrell of Ebbw Junction, pictured in 1947.
Note the cotton waste (or rag) in his hand.

when running through stations . . . and in populous neigh-bourhoods, particularly when near dwelling-houses'.[16]

Departure time for the 'Cornish Riviera Limited' was traditionally 10.30am. When the guard's whistle sounded down the platform, carriage doors were slammed shut and the signal indicator showed 'right away', allowing the driver to open the regulator and ease the great express out of the terminus. Building up speed slowly, the train would be travelling at about 60mph by the time it reached Ealing Broadway.

As the journey unfolded there would be little conversation between driver and fireman; aside from the sheer volume of noise being generated, the level of concentration required meant that both were intent on the task of keeping a 100-ton express locomotive and its train running safely at high speed and on time. In his 1937 article Driver Parsons emphasised the lack of conversation by noting that 'My fireman is far too busy keeping up steam and water, and I am almost glued to the eyeglass'[17]; the latter being a reference to the critical task of sighting signals. This was difficult enough when racing along the main line at 70mph in good weather but even more problematic in poor light, fog or smoke. Running trains in fog was particularly hazardous, and in the postwar years the great smogs that enveloped the main cities were terrible for footplate crews. Tom Conduit recalled the difficulties of running when the crew could not even see the ground from the cab of the locomotive, despite the fact that many engines were fitted with the ATC apparatus: distance and speed were difficult to calculate, especially as many engines were not fitted with speedometers. Worse still, when fog was very thick, the tops of the signal posts were invisible, and more than one driver has told of having to get down from the engine and climb up the signal ladder to see if the arm was at danger! In extreme conditions trains were cancelled, only a minimal passenger service being maintained. Footplate crew also hated working in snow and ice, especially when signal wires froze, making it difficult to tell if signal arms were showing the correct aspect.

It was during difficult conditions that the relationship between driver and fireman was put to the test. As all drivers will testify, the fear of hitting an obstruction on the line was foremost in the minds of footplate staff. At speed it was difficult to slow a heavily loaded train to avoid animals or persons on the line ahead without endangering the lives of the passengers, and those who had the misfortune to be driving when a trespasser or suicide victim was hit never forgot the experience. It was much more common for trains to come into contact with stray animals on the line; despite the best efforts of the Company in providing what it thought was secure fencing along its boundaries, animals did sometimes stray onto the permanent way. Company records from 1906 reveal that in that year 209 animals were killed

of the train and the number of carriages. While in the precincts of Brunel's great station at Paddington, the crew would do their best to ensure that the locomotive emitted no smoke; to this end, the driver might open the blower a touch and leave the fire door open. Minimising smoke was not only important to try and keep the station environment as clean as possible but, in the years after World War 2, was essential in the efforts being made generally to reduce smog within the capital. A British Railways notice issued by the Motive Power Department at Swindon in February 1950 warned drivers and firemen that local authorities were making efforts to reinforce the 1926 Public Health (Smoke Abatement) Act with additional by-laws and that it was 'not sufficient for Drivers and Firemen to take action to prevent the emission of smoke when engines are standing only, but they must also take care to prevent smoke being emitted

on the railway, of which sheep fared worst, 168 being killed; the toll also included 13 cattle, 12 pigs, 11 horses, four foxhounds and a solitary goat.

Racing along at 80mph on a non-stop express service like the 'Cornish Riviera Limited', the footplate crew had to perform a further operation, namely that of taking water. On the Great Western the tender of a locomotive was replenished by water troughs, which were situated at various locations around the network. On the main line west of Paddington the first troughs were at Pangbourne, although the 'Riviera' could also take water at Aldermaston (on the Berks & Hants line), at Cogload and at Exminster, in Devon. In most cases the troughs, laid between the rails, were between 500 and 600 yards long and were supplied with pre-softened water from a lineside pumping house. As the train approached the troughs the fireman would wind down a scoop attached to the tender, carefully judging the depth, to allow the water to surge into the tender. Examination of the top of Great Western tenders reveals a domed structure at the rear, designed to deflect water into the tender.

Just as there was considerable skill in allowing the scoop to skim the water of the troughs at the right depth, deft judgement was also needed to lift it at the correct moment when the tender was full. If the fireman were too slow or misread the gauge on the back of the tender, gallons of water could shoot out, flooding the first few compartments of the leading carriage. Ted Abear recalls travelling on a train in the 1940s from Paddington to Cardiff and warning a particularly insensitive passenger in his compartment who, even though it was March, insisted on having the window open, much to the discomfort of fellow passengers. As they left Reading, Ted, knowing that Goring Troughs were approaching, asked the passenger to close the window but was told in no uncertain terms that it was staying open. Ted and his companion then retired to the corridor, and, sure enough, when the train ran through the troughs, 'the scoop lifted a good proportion of the water through the window and into the lap of our friend, who spent the remainder of the journey trying to dry himself off'.[18]

Unlike the drivers of today, enclosed in heated cabs, footplate staff in the age of steam were very much at the mercy of the elements. Although later Collett and Hawksworth locomotives were built with large and fairly roomy cabs, many early Churchward and Dean designs were far more open to the weather, and in winter the crew had very little protection, especially when the wind was blowing across the cab, or, worse still, if the locomotive was running tender-first. In the latter instance, matters could be made worse by coal dust from the tender blowing back into the eyes of the driver and fireman. The Company thoughtfully provided a tarpaulin sheet, which could be stretched across from tender to cab, but this was not always entirely satisfactory. Weather aside, the crew faced other hazards; Ted Abear recalls vividly the experience of being in the cab of a steam locomotive while running along the line

Pride in the job simply oozes from the expression on the face of Driver Mann of Newton Abbot shed.

from Exeter to Newton Abbot. Leaving Exeter the railway runs along the sea wall through Dawlish and Teignmouth, and in winter the crew would crouch in the side of the cab as waves broke over the locomotive and carriages!

The condition of the engine could have a significant effect on the footplate crew, as already demonstrated by Bernard Barlow's experiences. When an engine was newly turned out from Swindon Works it could run very well; if it was a few miles short of an intermediate or heavy general overhaul, matters could be very different, and the crew could spend the journey being bounced around the cab. Certain classes of engine could be worse than others — not without good reason were the original 'County' 4-4-0s nicknamed 'Churchward's rough-riders'. J. W. Street, perhaps the most famous Great Western driver of the 1930s, noted that even his hairdresser had noticed the marks and small wounds on his head, caused by bumps sustained on a rough-riding locomotive.[19] Other classes, such as the 'Modified Halls', could also be a handful when in need of an overhaul. Some locomotives, meanwhile, seemed always to be shy of steam; others were always seen as good steamers. Every driver and fireman had his favourite and most-hated class, and the written reminiscences noted at the end of the book are full of tales that illustrate this.

Another hazard encountered by footplate staff was that of running through tunnels. Given that in steam days tunnels on busy stretches of line were seldom free from smoke and steam, being on the footplate of a slow, loose-coupled freight in a long tunnel could be a frightening and hazardous business. Harold Gasson recalled one such occasion on the footplate of 'ROD' 2-8-0 No 3030 between Honeybourne and Chipping Campden: the engine, already in poor condition, entered Honeybourne Tunnel, which was filled with black, oily smoke from the previous train; so thick was this that the crew, lying on the floor of the cab with wet handkerchiefs over their mouths in an effort to breathe relatively clean air, could see only by the glow of the firebox. Their ordeal worsened when the locomotive slipped on the greasy track inside the tunnel, reducing the train's speed to walking pace. As Harold remembered, 'That tunnel was only 887 yards in length, but it seemed as if it would go on for ever.'[20] The crew lived to tell the tale, and fortunately it was not always such an ordeal on the footplate. In this case driver and fireman stuck together and survived a particularly unpleasant experience.

Most retired staff remember working relationships on the footplate, and not always with affection. Tom Conduit

them; in the same way they tried to get the best from their firemen.

If working on the footplate on a long turn was bad enough, matters were made worse if crews were rostered to work a 'double home' or 'lodging turn'. On longer-distance goods workings particularly, the time and mileage involved meant that an overnight stay was required. For those with families or other commitments such turns were not welcome, although the accommodation provided did not make the proposition attractive for those without ties either! Staff were billeted either with landladies who regularly accommodated footplate staff or, in later years, in hostels provided by the railway. Ted Abear described the conditions in the 1950s at the hostel at Tyseley, nicknamed 'The Dogs' Home' by staff. Each room had three beds — one for the driver, one for the fireman, and one for the guard. Having experienced a particularly cold stay at the hostel, Ted and his mate made their next visit armed with hot water bottles to fight the freezing temperatures. Amazingly, they found themselves in trouble with the manageress, who told them they could not use their own hot water bottles without authority!

It is not the author's intention to recount in any detail a particular journey on the footplate of a Great Western or British Rail locomotive; many of the books noted in the sources at the end of this book give first-hand accounts of footplate trips, some exciting, some much less so. All, however, are recounted with an affection for the job shared by many railway staff. Writing in 1951, the outspoken but record-breaking driver J. W. Street, who had been in charge of many fast runs on the 'Cheltenham Flyer' and the 'Cornish Riviera Limited', noted that when he retired in 1936 he was proud to have been a Great Western man; he had never anticipated that the Company would be absorbed into British Railways, having imagined that the old Company would last 'a hundred years'.[21]

reckons that during his time as a fireman he probably worked with more than 20 different drivers, including some 'who couldn't drive a wheelbarrow!'. As is the case in all aspects of working life, past and present, there were some who could do the job but had a poor attitude and some who could not do the job but were good to work with. The best drivers, Tom remembered, were those who treated firemen like 'sons', looking after them and teaching them the tricks of the trade. With such attitudes, knowledge was passed easily from generation to generation of footplate staff. The best drivers also had an empathy with the locomotives they drove, treating them with respect and getting the best out of

An aerial view of the great works at Swindon recorded in 1922.

5

Inside Swindon Works

Before the railway came to Swindon, the quiet market town on the hill had little if any tradition of heavy engineering. When the Great Western Railway's workshops opened in 1843, most of the workforce had been brought in from areas where railway engineering was already strong — the North East of England, Manchester and Scotland. By the 1920s the descendants of those pioneering workers and their families were part of one of the largest railway communities in the United Kingdom.

This chapter will show what life was like for the people who worked in the factory that became world-famous as the place where, it was argued, they built the best railway engines in the world! Works and town were intertwined, and with over 12,000 employed by the railway at its height, it was not surprising that the shadow of the great works was cast far further than the tall imposing walls that surrounded it. The economic, social and political life of Swindon was dominated by the Great Western and, later, British Railways until well after World War 2 and the coming of other industry, like the Pressed Steel car plant, which offered alternative sources of employment.

Even today, the sheer size of the works remains difficult to comprehend; at its height it covered an area of over 323 acres, the vast enterprise dominated a whole swathe of the

A photograph taken shortly before World War 1, showing some of the thousands of men employed at the works walking down Rodbourne Road at lunchtime. The tram has had to halt until the crush abates.

centre of the town, from the railway station in the east to great 'A' Shop in the west, along the London–Bristol main line. The Gloucester branch bisected the Locomotive Works on the west side and the vast Carriage & Wagon Works to the east. To the south of the main line, facing the Railway Village, were further workshops, occupied by the Carriage & Wagon Department.

There was a marked divide between the Locomotive and Carriage & Wagon departments; each occupied a specific area of the works, and there was seldom movement from one trade to another amongst the workforce; indeed, on some occasions there was intense rivalry between departments. The division was exacerbated by the fact that areas of housing grew up around each department, populated by staff from those trades. Rodbourne, situated to the north of the Locomotive Works' great 'A' Erecting Shop, where many of the most famous GWR designs were assembled, was, not surprisingly, home to many 'locomotive side' staff, whilst in the east Gorse Hill was the province of 'carriage side' staff. Many retired staff remember that, in their childhood, battles were fought between gangs from each area, in the back alleys that criss-crossed the town! Within this chapter, the story of staff from both departments will be described to give an overall portrait of the railway community in Swindon.

Surrounding the factory were forbidding high stone or brick walls, which may have led to the expression used by Swindonians for being employed by the Great Western in the works: to work in the factory was to work 'inside' — a phrase which led to much confusion amongst newcomers to the town, who, overhearing it used in conversation, could be excused for thinking that someone was doing a stretch in one of HM's prisons!

The sense of community in the works was largely fostered by the way in which staff were employed; working 'inside' was very much a family affair, and today there are still many in the town who can trace their family history back through the generations, each being employed by the railway in some form or other. The town has changed dramatically in recent years, and the closure of the works in 1986 merely marked the last page in the final chapter of the works history, which saw its gradual decline from the town's biggest employer to a shadow of its former self, employing fewer than 3,000 staff when it finally shut for good.

The almost overwhelming dominance of the Great Western Railway meant that, for most boys, working in the railway works was an automatic career choice. John Fleetwood, who (as we shall discover later) spent his life working in the Foundry, confessed that as a boy he had harboured ambitions to be a motor mechanic but was told by his father that he had 'put him down to work in the factory', as indeed he had! Although teachers in local schools

Swindon apprentices sitting on the top of the Company's gasholder in the works, presumably without permission!
Bill Maynard

tried their best to steer those with academic ability away from the works, in the years of Depression before World War 2 many parents with large families simply could not afford to keep their sons in full-time education after the age of 14, and the works was a way of bringing in another valuable wage. Hugh Freebury, who joined the Great Western in 1932, had showed some promise at Elementary School but still decided to join his father, 'a second grade machineman "inside"', because his mother 'couldn't possibly afford to pay out for my education and keep us reasonably clothed and fed'.[1]

The influence of family has been mentioned more than once in this book, and in the case of the Great Western at Swindon the status of apprentices taken on by the Company would depend largely on the job held by their father. If their trade was a skilled one, it was likely that any sons would be given the choice of an apprenticeship in a similar field, although only two children from a family would be given this opportunity; any further children would be employed as labourers or in fitting, turning and erecting — the lowest rank of trade employed in the works.

Arthur Webb joined the service of the railway in 1934. His father had been employed in the Carriage & Wagon Works as a wood-wagon-builder, so when Arthur was offered an apprenticeship his options were limited. In the event, he was given the choice of an apprenticeship as a coach-trimmer or a blacksmith. He did not know what the first job entailed, but knew full well what the dirt, grime and discomfort of the latter involved and so elected to become a trimmer! The trimmer's job, as we will discover later in this chapter, involved the production and repair of coach upholstery and the laying of carpets and linoleum.

A GWR apprenticeship certificate signed by the Locomotive Superintendent, William Dean.

GREAT WESTERN RAILWAY.

LOCOMOTIVE & CARRIAGE DEPARTMENT,

ENGINEER'S OFFICE,

SWINDON, _21st Feby_ 1901

20531a

Certificate of Apprenticeship.

Name _Stephen Horatio Pugh_

Period of Apprenticeship _5 years from 17th Feb. 1896 to 16th Feb. 1901._

Where employed _Locomotive Works, Swindon_

Work on which employed

Work		Months
General Fitting & Machine Shop	Turning	14
" " " "	Fitting	25
Erecting Shop	General Repairs & Valve Setting	10
Millwrighting Shop	General Fitting	3
Testing House		7
Chemical Laboratory		1
		60 = 5 years.

YEAR ENDED		HOURS WORKS OPEN.	HOURS WORKED	TIME LOST (HOURS)				
				SPECIAL LEAVE	ILLNESS	WITHOUT LEAVE	TOTAL	
Feb	1897	2642	2460½	141¼	17¼	23	181½	
"	1898	2609¾	2212½	277½	110½	9¼	397¼	
"	1899	2533½	2339¾	187¼	–	6½	193¾	
"	1900	2629¼	2393	120	108	8¼	236¼	
"	1901	2636¾	2477½	156¼	–	3	159¼	
TOTALS ...		13,051¼	11,883¼	882¼	235¾	50	1168	x Includes 26 hours overtime

N.B.—The "Hours Works open" does not include the Works Holiday (averaging about 20 days per annum); "Special leave" represents time lost for Holidays in addition to the usual Works Holidays.

S. H. Pugh has satisfactorily completed an apprenticeship at these Works, as shewn by above table. He has always borne a very good character for diligent attention to his duties in the workshops, has been punctual and regular in his attendance, and the foremen, under whom he has been employed, report that he is a good workman.

Wm Dean

Chief Superintendent

G.W.R. Locomotive & Carriage Department.

On the locomotive side, the situation was much the same, with the best apprenticeships being out of the reach of most. Hugh Freebury's father, who, as already mentioned, was a 'Second Class Machineman', had earned just 40s per week, meaning that Hugh was denied the opportunity to learn his father's trade; had he been on the top grade, earning a further 2s per week, Hugh would have been able to follow in his father's footsteps. In the event, all Hugh was offered was boilermaking, considered 'more a disease than a trade' in Swindon.[2] For those able to afford the fee of £100 per year a 'Premium Apprenticeship' was available, offering the best training but requiring not only five years in the works but also the completion of academic studies in mechanical engineering.

Life for most ordinary 'trade' apprentices began in much the same way; since the Company would not employ boys when they first left school at 14, most had to find temporary employment outside the factory until they could start at the works. Hugh Freebury worked for a local bakery before getting the summons to start in the works at the age of 15. Arriving at the works, staff were normally allocated to a limited range of jobs before beginning their apprenticeship proper. The most popular posting was as an office boy; less attractive was the prospect of a stint as a 'rivet hotter' or a spell in the Bolt Shop.

For those beginning their life in the works as an office boy, their duties gave them a wonderful introduction both to the enormity of the works and to the range of activities carried out there. As well as the huge General Offices complex located at the end of the main subway into the works, almost all the individual workshops at Swindon had their own offices, and it was here that most office boys were first posted. On his first day, Arthur Webb was asked to report to the Road Wagon Shop, where horse-drawn road vehicles were built and maintained. This workshop was also identified by a number, as were all others in the Carriage & Wagon Department; Locomotive Department workshops were identified by letter.

One of the most important tasks carried out by an office boy was that of messenger, carrying correspondence from one workshop to another; Arthur Webb remembered that his route ran between the Road Wagon Shop, 5 Shop (train lighting), 16 Shop (wheel shop) and the large 24 Shop, where coach repairs took place. Collecting messages from the offices at each, he took them to the main Carriage & Wagon Department offices, where a series of leather bags marked with locations all over the factory hung on the wall of a corridor. Mail was then collected and delivered back to the Road Wagon Shop. For those with larger distances to cover, a number of bicycles were provided by the Company;

The Carriage & Wagon Works offices — one of the places visited by Arthur Webb as an office boy in the 1920s.

Machinists at work in 'R' Shop — now the STEAM museum — in the 1950s.

these were similar to those used by shopkeepers, with a large basket on the front. These heavy machines, with their small front wheels, must have been incredibly difficult for young office boys to manœuvre but must nevertheless have reduced wear and tear on their feet!

One of the concessions offered by the Company to its staff was that of reduced-price or 'Privilege' tickets on the railway itself, and another task performed by office boys involved the collection and delivery of such tickets. To obtain them, workmen needed a form, signed by the Shop Foreman, which was then taken to the Privilege Ticket Office, located just inside the works' main 'tunnel' entrance. As the office was only open for a few hours each morning and afternoon and for short periods after the end of the working day, office boys were sent to go and collect the tickets; workmen gave them the cost of the tickets and usually paid them a few coppers for their trouble. Although this was not strictly part of an office boy's duties, foremen and management turned a blind eye to the practice, which had been a feature of life in the factory for years.

Many former office boys have fond memories of Christmas, when they were allowed to circulate a Christmas box amongst the staff in the workshop. Arthur Webb recalled that, although there were a number of washers in the box, he was taken aback to find that his more senior workmates had between them donated over £3 — almost enough for him to be able to purchase a bicycle, which he would use to get to work in the morning. Amazingly, the bike he bought in a shop in nearby Bridge Street for £3 10s in 1936 served him faithfully until 1967!

Despite the strict discipline within the workshops, it was inevitable that some of the young boys employed would get up to mischief. The fact that office boys could wander around the works whilst taking post and other correspondence around the site meant that they often had the opportunity to loiter — something which did not escape the attention of the management. In August 1922 R. G. Hannington, the Locomotive Works Manager, sent all his foremen a private circular noting that his attention had been 'continually drawn' to 'the slackness which prevails amongst the Office Boys employed in the Works', the chief shop clerks being requested to 'take the lads in hand with a view to improve matters'.[3] His solution to the problem was to ask each office boy to record how long he took on each errand, in order that anyone idling could be reprimanded! The problem was clearly ongoing, however, as in November 1925 another circular was issued following a complaint from none other than the Chief Mechanical Engineer concerning the number of 'boys continually going in and out of the Factory'.

For other junior members of staff starting in the factory, their first job was much less pleasant. Being posted to the 'Scraggery', situated on the ground floor of the 'R' Machine Shop, meant working in a building full of small furnaces, where steel rod was heated and then fed through a series of presses which produced blank nuts or bolts. After cooling, these would be threaded by more skilled staff, but the top and bottom of the bolt also needed to be 'scragged' or faced off. This operation was perhaps one of the most basic of machining tasks but was a good introduction to the feel of machine tools for the young apprentice. Nuts and bolts removed from locomotives under repair would also be cleaned of the grease and muck with which they had become coated and prepared for reuse. As a result the Scraggery, presided over by chargehand Harry Turner, is still remembered by many Swindon staff today as an extremely unpleasant place, where they not only had to contend with the dirt and grime but also suffered cuts, abrasions and bruises from the hard manual work into which they were plunged at a tender age.

Most young staff were offered a 'Trade' or proper apprenticeship after an initial period of a year or so, and it was from this point on that they learned the basics of the trade they were to follow. It should be noted at this point, however, that the offer of an apprenticeship was not a guarantee of long-term continuing employment. Once the five-year training had been completed, to the satisfaction of the Company, apprentices had to endure an anxious time before discovering if they had been retained or 'let go' by the GWR. Many who had received high-quality training,

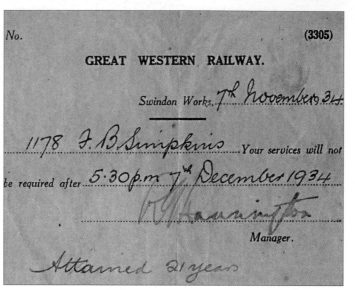

The note dreaded by apprentices — the slip informing them that their services were no longer required.

particularly in the difficult years of the Depression, were forced to seek employment away from the town, largely because there was little other heavy-engineering activity nearby. However, the cachet of a Swindon apprenticeship was quite often a passport to a job in the Merchant Navy or with other large engineering companies, as well as a virtual guarantee of a position on a railway in one of Britain's overseas colonies or dependencies.

The beginning of the working day was always marked by the mournful howl of the famous Swindon Works hooters that summoned the men to the factory. In the early days, when most staff lived in the 300 or so houses that comprised the Railway Village, the Great Western employed a man to walk up and down the deserted streets early each morning, ringing a hand bell to wake the men (and their families), in the same manner as the 'knocker-ups' described in the chapter on locomotive-cleaners. Later still, a bell was mounted on the roof of 'C' Shop in the works itself.

As the works grew during the course of the 19th century, and waves of terraced red-brick houses were built by speculative builders away from the Railway Village and Factory, something more powerful was required to regulate the working day. Hooters (quaintly described at the time as 'steam trumpets') were installed and over the years were situated in a number of locations, finally being fixed to the top of the Hydraulic Power House, close to the huge 'V' Boiler Shop in the Locomotive Works. A member of staff was employed to blow the hooter over an hour before the start of work each morning, which meant that in the latter part of the 19th century the inhabitants of Swindon were subjected to a 10-minute blast at 5.20am! The hooter was also sounded at intervals up to the beginning of the shift, as well as at lunchtime and at the end of the day. As the works contracted in size during the latter part of the 20th century, the volume of the hooters diminished somewhat, but just how loud they were in the heyday of Swindon can be judged by the fact that they could be heard well over a dozen miles away, even being audible (with a following wind) in places like Stow-on-the-Wold in the Cotswolds!

The hooter being sounded by a member of works staff shortly before closure.
The valuable GWR drop-dial clock had by this time been removed for safety. *Roy Nash*

The power of the hooters was for good reason; by 1900 staff were coming to work not only from the immediate area around the workshops but also from surrounding villages. Special workmen's trains were run via a number of routes: west of Swindon, along the Bristol–London main line, men came from the village of Wootton Bassett; those living in locations on the Swindon–Gloucester route, such as Purton and Minety, were also catered for, as were those on the old Midland & South Western Junction route and the Highworth branch line. For staff living in villages like Lydiard, South Marston or Wroughton, until the coming of bus services in the 20th century there was little choice but to walk or cycle to work. One can but admire those workers who in the 19th century walked four or five miles to the Factory, completed a strenuous eight- or nine-hour shift and then walked home again at night — a routine they repeated in all weathers, six days a week, as at that time staff worked on Saturday mornings.

On commencing service with the Company every member of staff employed at the workshops was issued with a small navy-blue rulebook. A glance at its dozen or so pages provides a fascinating insight into the discipline and management style practised by the Great Western at Swindon. Although, in the course of the 20th century, rules were relaxed and modified, overall discipline remained strict until well after World War 2. According to the 1904 edition, staff were expected to work a 54-hour week, as follows:

Monday to Friday:	6am to 8.15am
	9am to 1pm
	2pm to 5.30pm
Saturday:	6am to 8.15am
	9am to 12 noon

At this time staff stopped for a breakfast break at 8.15am; although most brought their own food with them, local establishments grew up around the works to cater for staff, and the nearby Rodbourne Coffee Tavern in Rodbourne Road offered a 'Workman's Breakfast' for 2d. The rulebook also noted that staff were entitled to overtime, although only at time-and-a-quarter up to 10pm, after which time-and-a-half was payable.

With the sound of the last hooter dying away, the watchmen slammed the large wooden doors at each entrance firmly shut. The staff employed at the entrances were usually (although not exclusively) staff who had been

An atmospheric view of one of the offices at Swindon Works, with an impressive collection of bonnets and hats hung on the wall!

moved there after illness or accident had prevented them from carrying out their normal duties. As well as keeping out unwanted visitors or representatives without an appointment, they patrolled the works site and carried out spot checks to ensure that staff were not pilfering from the works. Inevitably, resourceful workers found all manner of creative ways to sneak material out of the site; one particular ruse was the manufacture of duffel bags made to the exact diameter of paint tins, allowing half-finished tins to be brought out of the works without suspicion. As at all large industrial undertakings, it was common for jobs to be done in the workshops by staff for their colleagues. Known as 'foreigners', anything from clothes-line poles (made from old boiler tubes) to coffee tables and even entire greenhouses were made in the works and smuggled out under the noses of the watchmen. On top of this, staff could also purchase scrap material at ludicrously low prices; indeed, such was the amount of Company material in workers' houses, it was said that when the hooter blew, half of Swindon shivered!

The Company held staff punctuality as being of paramount importance. It was not sufficient for workers merely to arrive at the works by the time the final hooter sounded, as by this time they were expected to be at their respective workplaces. An unusual and distinctive method for recording attendance and timekeeping was adopted, using brass time 'checks', each stamped with a number unique to each workman; at the beginning of the day each would hang his check on a board with numbered hooks, in front of which a member of staff (nicknamed the 'checky') would bring down a glass window when the final hooter sounded. Staff arriving late without good cause would usually be fined according to how late they were. Anyone arriving up to 15 minutes late had this amount docked from his pay, and a green-painted $\frac{1}{4}$ check was placed on his hook to mark the offence. Greater punishment awaited those turning up even later; persistent lateness could lead to dismissal — a sobering prospect in what was effectively a one-company town where a railway job meant more than job security and its loss would mean the loss of subsidised travel, coal and medical treatment. The check system was abandoned only in the 1970s, when a more conventional card-operated electric-time-clock system was installed.

The works was managed and administered largely from the General Offices, an imposing three-storey building situated at the end of the main subway and overlooking the tangle of railway lines connecting the factory with the Great

100

Pay day at Swindon in the 1980s. Staff were using the same pay tables as had been used by their GWR forebears in the 1930s!
Roy Nash

Western main line to the east; additional offices for the Loco-motive and Carriage Works managers were located elsewhere on the site. Before being employed, clerks were required to sit an examination, as well as undergoing the normal medical examination and receiving a recommendation from a family member already employed by the Company.

Few women had been employed in the works — let alone the offices — until World War 1, when many men joined the armed forces. The consequent shortage of skilled staff led the Company to employ women in large numbers, although this decision aroused great debate amongst the staff generally. The *Great Western Railway Magazine* printed a number of letters that in the modern era seem almost quaint, one writer noting in 1915 that 'when left to herself to deal with a question the female clerk does not show any aptitude for grasping the subject.'[4]

Despite all the debate, after the war women continued to be employed in large numbers, albeit paid at a lower rate than were their male counterparts. A glance at a 1939 contract for a female clerk reveals that at 16 years of age a woman could expect to be paid 17s 6d per week, this rising to 35s at 21 and reaching a maximum of 60s per week at 30; however, most female staff would not reach this last figure, as the contract stipulated that 'Retirement from the Service is compulsory on marriage.'

In coping with the level of administration necessary at a large works like Swindon, staff had few of the advantages enjoyed by today's office workers. Information was recorded laboriously by hand in large ledgers or card indexes, and, although clerks would eventually have the use of primitive adding machines (then known as comptometers), much of the statistical and mathematical work was done by staff with a good head for figures!

One of the week's most important tasks was the payment of the 12,000 or so staff. Until the 1980s many staff were paid in cash, and, once the amount for each worker had been calculated, a request was made for the cash to Lloyds' Bank in Regent Street. On Thursday morning the money was collected from the bank in a specially made armoured wagon manufactured from boiler plate in 'L2' Shop. Having been loaded with the wages, the horse-drawn wagon returned to the works by the same route each week, escorted by half a dozen staff, each carrying a pickaxe handle for protection! There followed the laborious task of sorting out the cash for each employee, the money being placed in a small steel tin that was then distributed to each member of staff on Friday morning. Specially made Pay Tables were erected in each workshop, and staff from the wages office came and paid out the money, having received from each man a copper pay check similar to the time checks described earlier. This ritual continued until closure of the works in 1986, even though the steel tins had by then been replaced by more familiar paper wage packets.

There is not space in this chapter to describe all the many and various trades practised in the works, so a number of the more interesting have been chosen. Away from the offices, working conditions varied widely within the workshops, depending greatly on the type of job being done. Conditions were worst in the 'hot' shops, those involving processes such as blacksmithing, casting and the like. Jack Hayward, who began his career well after World War 2, in January 1956, nevertheless described the sense of shock he felt on his first day when he was taken from the relative calm of the Staff Office in the General Offices to the shop office in the nearby Spring Shop, where he was to start his new job as a clerk.[5] Right up until closure in 1986, the works produced leaf and coil springs for locomotives, using techniques little changed over the years. It was no wonder, then, that Jack felt that the scene before him resembled something from the Victorian era, with lines of furnaces serving the scores of staff turning out this most valuable of commodity to the railway industry. Following the Chief Clerk down the workshop, Jack described the building as being full of fumes given off by the furnaces — a situation compounded by the dust rising from the ash-covered floor. A shower of sparks emanating from huge circular saws added to the din made by steam hammers and the clamour of the men in the workshop. All in all, Jack's experience constituted truly a 'baptism of fire' and one he was not sure he should repeat; going home at lunchtime, he told his parents that he had no intention of returning, but, as a railway family, they reassured him that all would eventually be well and calmed him down.

Despite the awful conditions prevailing in the workshop, the blacksmiths employed there were able to produce work of an extremely high standard, including coupling hooks and links, drawbars and various hand tools such as the long

firing irons used by the footplate staff (as described in Chapter 4). As well as conventional anvils, blacksmiths used steam and drop hammers to shape larger steel forgings. Each hammer was manned by a blacksmith, who 'drove' or controlled it, a 'striker', who wielded a 7lb sledgehammer, and a labourer. Jack Hayward noted that 'once the job was under the hammer, the three of them worked in unison before the red hot metal cooled'. Close by were the furnaces, tended by a member of staff to maintain the high temperatures needed, as many forgings had to be heated and reheated before they were complete; in later years these were gas-powered, but in the 1950s coke was still needed to keep them working. Also dotted around the workshop were 'boshes' — large tanks of filthy oily water used to temper and cool the steel once it had been forged.

Close to the Blacksmiths' Shop was the Steam Hammer Shop proper, where much larger forgings were cast. Indeed, such were the size of these that hoists were required to lift them into position and hold them steady while the hammers did their work. Large 'drop' hammers were utilised whereby the huge top block was raised by steam pressure and then released in free fall, delivering a 50-ton blow to the forging. After each blow the men would manoeuvre the steel billet ready for the next. A blow from the hammer shook everything around it, and Swindonians can recall even today how the ground vibrated well away from the workshop where the great hammers operated. The work of the hammer-men normally featured on any tour of the works, and skilled hammer-drivers would demonstrate their control by putting an open matchbox on the hammer anvil and bringing the hammer down closer and closer to the box until the stroke could gently close it without damage. For those brave enough the tour guide would ask for a volunteer to place his or her wristwatch on the anvil and watch as the hammer moved up and down within a hair's breadth of its glass face. How many replacements the Company had to provide over the years is not recorded!

In his role as a clerk in the Shop Office serving the Blacksmiths', Steam Hammer and Bolt shops, Jack Hayward was able to record memories of not only processes and working conditions but also his workmates. One character he described typified the appearance of the Swindon workman in the 20th century — the office messenger, who, it was claimed, was 64 years old. He was almost certainly older than this and must have started his career in the works

The Spring Shop in 1984. The machines and the general atmosphere are such that this picture could have been taken 50 years earlier! *Roy Nash*

Above:
The Blacksmith's Shop at Swindon, with hearths visible either side and the drop hammers in the centre.

Right:
One of the largest steam hammers. No wonder the ground shook violently when these machines were in action!

during the Great War. He was dressed in 'thick black worsted trousers, with ever shiny seat and knees, white linen shirt, rolled up sleeves with no collar; on top of this he wore the traditional black worsted waistcoat with silk back'. The Great Western did not generally provide overalls or uniforms for staff in the railway works, and staff were responsible for providing their own, usually in the pattern described by Jack, or utilising an old pin-striped suit; countless photographs of the workshops seem to bear this out. The only exceptions were the provision of specialist protective aprons or overalls in workshops like the Blacksmiths' Shop and the supply of heavy-duty clogs or boots in some locations, as usual stamped with the Company initials. Such heavy and ungainly footwear was made even more awkward by the addition of heavy-duty metal studs on the soles and heels.

After some years Jack applied for a new position to broaden his experience. The location of his new job was in the offices of the Foundry, next to the Bristol–London

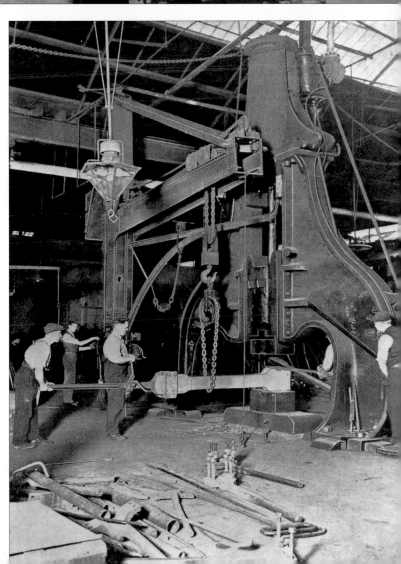

Two atmospheric views of moulds being poured in the Foundry, during manufacture of a large special casting for the railway works' Boiler Shop.
Bill Wheeler collection

main line. If conditions in the Blacksmiths' Shop had seemed Dickensian, then the environment of the Foundry was, if anything, worse. Until the end of the steam era the Foundry was divided into three, each with its own particular function. The Iron Foundry was the largest and produced ferrous castings such as locomotive cylinders, chimneys, wheels and other fittings. The Brass Foundry, located close by, produced non-ferrous castings such as injectors and other smaller engine fittings in metals like brass and bronze; also produced here were the letters and numbers used on the name- and numberplates so prized by railway collectors today. Finally, the 'Chair' Foundry was used to manufacture the cast-iron track chairs of all shapes and sizes used by the Permanent Way Department.

John Fleetwood spent his entire 40-year railway career in the Foundry, finishing as Head Foreman. His father had been employed as a tractor-driver, moving material around the works site, and as such was classed by the Great Western as

'semi-skilled'. This meant that the range of apprenticeships offered to John was limited to the trades of moulder, rough painter and machinist; as the job of moulder paid 2s per week more than the others, he elected to do this, much to the displeasure of his mother.

Like others described earlier, John had begun work at 15 in the Scraggery facing and threading nuts and bolts, and although the Foundry was literally five minutes' walk from there, nothing prepared him for the inside of this workshop, which he described as a 'black dirty hole'. That this came as such a surprise was due to the fact that, at that time, staff were not encouraged to wander around the works, and

anyone apart from an office boy, who would have permission to move freely around the 300-acre site, was likely to incur the wrath of a foreman or chargeman if not in his own workshop.

The training John Fleetwood received was typical of the way in which apprentices learned their trade in the works, with the exception of 'Premium' apprentices, who had a better grounding in the theory of railway engineering, largely because they undertook additional training in the evening at the Technical School in Victoria Road. Most apprentices learned very much on the job, listening and watching older and wiser staff who passed on their skill and knowledge to new entrants. The apprenticeship took five years to complete, and in the case of the Foundry, this broke down into a stint in each of the Iron and Brass foundries. The time was not divided equally, and John remembered that he worked for about nine months at a time in one location before being moved to the other. He started by working with an experienced and skilled moulder, who, he recalled, was not afraid to 'cuff him around the ear' if he got things wrong!

As a moulder, John had the job of preparing the moulds used to make the castings. On a typical day the first task was to mix up the moulding sand — a dusty and messy job. Exactly how much sand was prepared depended largely on the size of the castings being manufactured and the amount of work being done. It was said that horse dung was used as the secret ingredient to bind together the sand, although in reality John remembers this being used only for certain jobs, the dung aerating the sand and thus allowing gases given off by the hot metal to escape more easily. Once this job was complete, moulding boxes were made up for the items to be cast. The wooden pattern of the item to be cast was placed inside one of these boxes, which was then packed with sand, forced in hard; the pattern was then removed, leaving its impression in the sand. The two halves of the mould thus created were combined, and various other holes, to allow the passage of the molten metal in and fumes and air out, made in the sand. For small runs of components all the work was done by hand, but for repetitious and well-used items such as brake blocks or fire bars, which were manufactured in their hundreds, machine moulders did the work.

By the middle of the day there would be literally dozens of moulding boxes placed in rows in the workshop, waiting to be filled with molten metal. Once the day's moulding work was complete, the task of pouring the moulds began. Cupolas, wherein the molten metal was produced, were located behind the north wall of the Foundry and could produce around 10 tons of cast iron per hour, heating it to a temperature of about 1,300°C. From around 11.45am staff began the task of filling containers, known by the men as 'ladles', with the molten iron. Depending on the amount of work to be done, a ladle could be carried down the iron-plate floor of the workshop by two men, carrying it

between them. The task of carrying this 80lb container could be perilous; if they dawdled, the hot metal could eat its way through the sides or bottom of the container and leak out; ladles were lined with red sand to slow this process, but basically staff needed to be quick! Larger 'prams' — 5cwt ladles mounted on a two-wheeled trolley — could be used for larger, repetitive runs of castings. For extremely big jobs, huge ladles suspended from the overhead cranes that ran the length of the workshop were used.

Once all the moulds had been cast, it remained for staff to 'knock out' the castings — removing the completed components from the moulding boxes — ready for the night shift to collect. The final task before the hooter blew for the last time that day was to damp down the sand with water. John Fleetwood described the work as 'hot and dirty', and with so much sand around, it was not surprising that he went home each day 'as black as a chimney sweep'.

Until more modern times, washing facilities were (to say the least) primitive — a situation repeated all over the railway works. In the Foundry there was merely a large trough, shared by 40 men; to make matters worse, as well as the Company-supplied 'sand soap', which was 'rough enough to rub the skin off your face', there were only six towels, which had to last them all week! Some idea of the

A cylinder mould almost complete in the Foundry, in a picture taken in 1951.

condition of these troughs can be gained from a circular, issued to foremen in March 1923, which noted that some were 'in a very dirty condition'; the Works Manager instructed foremen that the washing troughs be 'periodically scrubbed by your shop labourers' to rectify the situation.[6] After World War 2, with the advent of Health & Safety legislation, matters improved, and eventually Foundry staff had access to proper toilets and even showers — facilities their forebears could scarcely have conceived of! It is not difficult to imagine how hot the Foundry must have been in summer, particularly when casting was taking place; less well-known is how cold the workshops were in the winter, with no direct heating. On one very cold morning, when even the water in buckets in the Foundry was freezing, John Fleetwood decided to risk the wrath of the foreman by asking about the lack of heating. The answer came that, if he was cold, he was obviously not working hard enough!

Conditions within the Brass Foundry were much worse than those in the Iron Foundry, largely because fumes given off during the casting of yellow brass were far more toxic. Lack of an extraction system within the building meant that the whole place was filled with clouds of choking, acrid smoke. Two cases of suspected lead poisoning in the years after World War 2 led the railway to take action: a fume-extraction system was installed, and regular health checks were introduced for staff working there; in addition, workmen were encouraged to drink a pint of milk a day to combat the lead.

One aspect of his career in the works that John Fleetwood remembered with little affection was that of working the night shift. He described the first night as being particularly bad, since he had not slept during the day before, believing he could manage without sleep — a decision he regretted as the night wore on. It was during the night that the rats, which infested the works, were very active. Les Mace, interviewed in the 1980s, remembered that they fed on the grease on pulley blocks and on workmen's food, if the men were foolish enough to leave it lying about; on the night shift, he was convinced that one particular rodent ran down a hot pipe at the same time each night: 'You could almost set your watch by it,' he remembered.[7] To try and keep the problem under control the men brought in cats, which not surprisingly bred, so that soon there were cats in almost every workshop, roaming the whole site. The author, visiting the works just before closure in 1986, saw many cats still living in the workshops, cared for by the men; when the end finally came for Swindon, most were taken home with redundant staff, even though some were feral animals by then.

Away from the 'hot shops' conditions were very different; in the various machine shops the work was no less hard but required different skills and capabilities. One of the most common apprenticeships undertaken was that of fitting and turning, which trained staff to use the many and various machine tools used to produce finished components from the rough castings or forgings manufactured in the Foundry or Blacksmiths' Shop. Lathes, drilling machines, slotters, grinders and all manner of other specialised machine tools were required for this task, and until well after World War 2 many ran off overhead 'line shafting' powered by a stationary steam engine situated outside the workshop. Large belts ran from this shafting to each individual machine, and quite often a number of machines ran off the same shafting. This meant that, if a belt snapped or another problem arose, all the machines in the group stopped, giving staff a breather, although, as many remember, the shop foreman or chargehand would soon be on the scene to ensure that staff were not slacking. Even if the belts had stopped, staff were expected to clean or lubricate their lathe in the down-time.

Accidents were not uncommon within the machine shops. With so many belts and moving parts, the opportunities for mishaps were high, especially in the years before Health & Safety legislation dictated that guards and other equipment be installed to give some protection to the workers. For some men who had long worked without guards, the new measures were clearly seen as a nuisance, and a 1936 booklet, 'Safety Precautions for Railway Shopmen', warned that guards should not be removed: 'It is

A graphic illustration of why it was recommended that staff wear safety goggles when using machines.

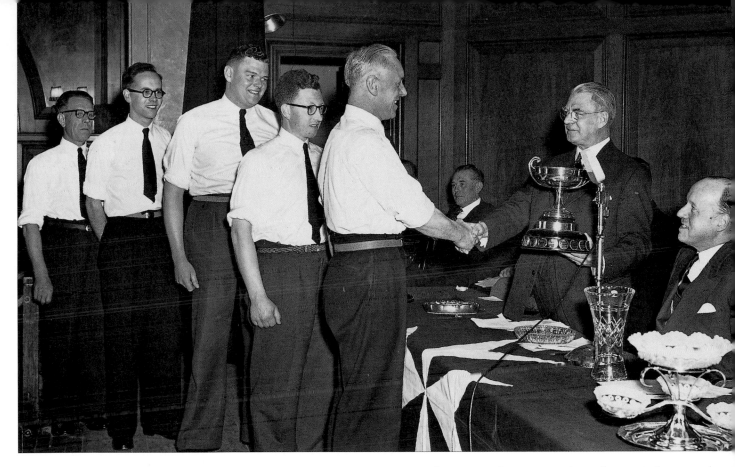

The Swindon 'B' St John Ambulance team receiving a First Aid trophy from WR Chairman R. F. Hanks in 1956.

plain common sense to use them.' The fact that such a warning was necessary can be gleaned from a circular issued by the Locomotive Works Manager in December 1922, which noted that he had learned that the safety guard on a number of portable electric grinding machines had been removed and that 'this may result in a serious accident'. The 1936 booklet further warned: 'Many a serious accident has resulted from unsuitable clothing worn by men operating lathes and other machines . . . Jackets should be made to button tightly'; it also recommended that cuffs on jackets be buttoned tightly around the wrist.

Aside from the danger of catching clothes in high-speed lathes or other equipment in the machine shop was that of injury to the eyes. Use of such machines entailed a high probability of chippings or metal turnings flying off and injuring workmen. The Great Western (and, later, British Railways) laid down strict instructions that goggles be worn 'in all cases where there is a risk to the eyes'. Staff were issued with small metal safety goggles which were made in the workshops, but many found them uncomfortable and difficult to wear and took their chances without them. Writing to all senior staff in the Locomotive Department in August 1923, Chief Mechanical Engineer C. B. Collett

noted that 'the number of eye accidents in these works is disturbing, and I shall be glad if you will instruct your Foremen to give the matter close and constant attention'. The adoption of protective measures after a serious accident was no good, he argued. Interestingly, given that Health & Safety legislation was in its infancy, Collett identified the fact that the men were left to decide whether to use goggles or not, thereby leaving them open to injury. The decision, he wrote, 'should not be left to their determination alone'. In later years the enforcement of such measures would become mandatory.

One further measure that assisted in the maintenance of Health & Safety within the works was the involvement of the workforce in the First Aid movement. The provision of emergency first aid by the men themselves was, as in other parts of the railway, made possible by training and guidance provided by the Order of St John. Every workshop had at least one wooden First Aid box (in British Railways days painted green), to which all qualified St John Ambulance Brigade volunteers had a key. Inside was enough equipment to allow an accident victim to be stabilised before being taken by stretcher to the Great Western Hospital in Emlyn Square. Regular classes were held, and teams from Swindon

Works competed in the many regional and national competitions which were held by the Great Western (and, later, British Railways). Swindon staff also had the advantage of being members of the Great Western Medical Fund Society, a 'cradle to grave' health scheme funded by contributions from their wages. Set up as early as 1848, this gave them access to a wide variety of high-quality medical treatment and other important facilities like swimming baths, Turkish baths and a pharmacy. When the National Health Service was being set up after World War 2 the Great Western Medical Fund was used as an example of good practice by Ernest Bevin, the minister in charge.

Mention of the foreman naturally leads to further discussion of the strict regime under which Swindon workers were employed. As most retired staff will confirm, the foreman was 'God' and not someone to cross without good reason. The 'badge of office' was of course the bowler hat, although this was partly replaced in the 1930s by the trilby. Most foremen were strict disciplinarians and, having come up through the ranks themselves, were more than aware of the tricks and dodges practised by their men. Whilst most engendered (sometimes grudging) respect from their staff, there were some who were judged to have been promoted above their station and who, it was felt, needed cutting down to size. An apocryphal story tells of a foreman, promoted from the ranks, who had become 'too big for his boots'. Coming in to work each day, he always swapped the bowler he wore outside the works for another, presumably more worn, for use at work. Staff in the workshop substituted this with one two sizes too small, which, when the foreman put it on, perched on top of his head. Not wishing to lose face, he carried on wearing it for the whole day. The next morning it had been replaced with a hat two sizes bigger than his regular bowler, so he was forced to shove newspaper in it to prevent it from slipping down. There the prank ended, the workers having made their point, but one wonders whether the foreman got his revenge eventually!

Foremen and chargemen obviously kept a close eye on staff; it was no coincidence that, in most parts of the works, offices had large glazed screens fronting the workshop, allowing them to see that all staff were applying themselves to the job in hand. Chargemen, who were responsible for individual gangs of men within each workshop, had large wooden boxes, big enough to have an inclined desk within them, where piecework calculations could be made. Most boxes were fitted with mirrors, allowing chargemen to see what was going on behind their back. Supervisory staff even policed toilet breaks: in bigger workshops a member of staff was seated outside toilets, and workmen had to hand in their time checks when entering; if they stayed longer than 10 minutes they risked losing pay; John Fleetwood remembered a 'low-paid chap' who sat in a little office outside the toilets, shouting 'Your time is up!' when the 10 minutes had elapsed!

The whole subject of piecework was one of the most contentious issues within the workshops. Applying to many workshops in both the Locomotive and Carriage & Wagon departments, it was based on the concept that every job done had a price which had been calculated by the Company and recorded in a register. Arthur Webb recalled

that in his day the bonus or 'balance' was paid fortnightly, alternating with a week of basic pay. The amount of piecework was calculated by the foreman or chargeman, and how much work had been done — and thus the balance paid — could vary. Some retired railway staff were convinced that, if a foreman took a dislike to a member of staff or a gang, he could dispute or reduce the amount of piecework bonus paid, with serious consequences to the men involved, who, although well paid by the standards of other workers, such as those in agriculture, still had bills to pay and children to feed and clothe. It paid not to cross one's foreman, as he had the power to make life very difficult.

Most railway historians and enthusiasts with some knowledge of Great Western locomotives agree that one of the key strengths of Swindon engines was their free-steaming and powerful boiler design. No doubt much of this success was due to the advances in design made by locomotive engineers such as G. J. Churchward and the teams of draughtsmen and technical staff employed in the Drawing Office, but considerable credit must also be given to the workmen who built and maintained the boilers in working conditions we would now consider intolerable.

As Alfred Williams noted in his book *Life in a Railway Factory*, published in 1915, although boiler-making staff might not have been as skilled individually as fitters or other workers elsewhere at Swindon, as a group they were essential to the needs of the Company. The particular skills they practised made theirs 'an exclusive profession', as the construction of the boiler was both an expensive and a difficult job.[8] Boilers cost almost £1,000 each and took up to six months to complete. The quality of workmanship had always to be of the highest order; there could be no mistakes or shoddy finishing, for the consequences of a bodged job could be disastrous for a locomotive crew.

There were two main categories of boilermaker — the platers and the riveters. The former were responsible for preparing, marking off and cutting out the boiler plate as well as supervising the drilling of holes where required. The riveters completed the construction process by riveting together the various parts of the boiler. When Williams wrote about the Boiler Shop in 1915, much of the riveting was done laboriously by hand, with apprentices or labourers heating up the rivets in small furnaces and throwing them up to the riveters to fix into position. By the 1930s, however, the Company was using hydraulic riveting equipment, which speeded up the whole construction process considerably.

The noise experienced in various locations around the works was as nothing compared to the wall of sound confronting a visitor to the Boiler Shop. This might well contain more than 200 boilers — a mixture of new work and those in for repair, having been removed from locomotives when they were brought in for overhaul. During the steam era at Swindon anything up to 500 boiler-makers

The Boiler Shop Stores, seen in 1928. Visible in this picture are rivets, stays and boiler-washout plugs.

might be at work in this vast building, most hammering, riveting or crawling over the boilers that lay in various positions and states of repair all over the shop. As Williams reported, literally hundreds of hand and machine tools would be in use at any one time, and the din would have been unimaginable to anyone who did not have the misfortune to work there.

Such was the noise that staff working there made little attempt to talk to each other, save by shouting directly into a colleague's ear. Instead, the workers communicated largely by sign language — the only way they could make themselves understood. One apprentice who began his working life in the Boiler Shop also discovered that, although it was a noisy place to work, foremen still managed to keep an eye on errant staff. Having been told off for a minor transgression and walking away from the foreman, he swore in frustration, and as he moved further away he received a cuff around the ear! Bravely asking the foreman what the blow was for, he was firmly told that whilst noise levels in the shop were

high, it did not prevent supervisory staff from mastering the art of lip-reading!

Despite such high noise levels there was little attempt in the steam era to protect the hearing of staff working there from damage. As already observed, Health & Safety legislation was limited until well after World War 2, and as a result most boiler-makers were prematurely deaf by the age of 30. Jack Hayward says that, even today, one can identify retired staff who had worked in the Boiler Shop from the fact that virtually all of them now wear hearing aids! It was perhaps for this reason too that, at Swindon, boiler-makers were known as 'fitters with their brains knocked out'.

Perhaps the largest concentration of men in the works was in the huge 'A' Erecting Shop, situated at the western end of the site, next to the main Bristol–London railway line. Construction of the workshop had begun in 1900 and continued until after World War 1; when completed in 1923 it was one of the largest and most modern locomotive

A New Work programme sheet, detailing the various workshops involved in building an engine at the works.

New Work Programme No.17.

Lot 228. 9th. five.   Engines 5640 – 5644

	Principal Shops concerned						Date reqd. in Erecting Shop
Main Frames & A.I. Stiffeners				V	Q	W	30-6-25
Dragbar box frames				V	Q	W	"
Cylinders	J					W	17-7-25
Hornblocks & Hornties	J	F				W	AM "
Motion plates							AM 18-7-25
Valve Spindle Crosshead Guides	J			V	Q		AM "
Hanging bars & Radial Guides				V	Q.	W	AM 20-7-25
Buffer bars & frame brackets				V	Q	W	"
Spring Hanger brackets		St				R	"
Brake " "		St					AM "
Motion bars		F					AM 24-7-25
Reversing shafts & brackets	J	F					AM 28-7-25
Brake shafts & B.		F					AM "
Vacuum cylinders & reservoirs	J			V	Q		AM "
Boilers				V			1-8-25
Smokeboxes			L2	V		W	"
Expansion brackets		F				W	"
Axleboxes							AM 5-8-25
Wheels							AW "
Eccentric sheaves & straps	J	St	F				AM 6-8-25
Radial trucks	J						AM 10-8-25
Lifeguards & stays				V	Q		AM "
Coupling rods	U	F					AM 13-8-25
Connecting rods	U	F					AM "
Sandboxes & gear		St	F L2	Q			AM "
Springs		Sp				R	15-8-25
Spring hangers & gear		St					AM "
Reversing gear		F					AM "
Valve gear		St	F				AM "
Ashpans			L2	Q			"
Pistons & crossheads, vacuum pumps	J					R	AM "
" packings, rings & glands	J	Sp				R	"
Piston valves	J	St					AM "
" " rings & glands	U	Sp				R	"
Relief valves & air valves	U					T	"
Steam pipes	K	St				W	"
Blast pipes & chimneys	J						AM 18-8-25
Tanks			L2	Q			20-8-25
" levelling pipes	J						AM "
" feed cocks & empty cocks	J					T	"
Injectors & pipes	K U					T	24-8-25
Cylinder cocks & gear	U	St F		V	Q		AM "
Lubricators T.S.F. & Syphon cups	J	U				T	"
Ejectors	U					T	"
Handrails & pillars	K					R	"
Buffers	B						"
Draw gear	B						"
Number plates	J						"
Trial							5-9-25 to 19-9-25

Castings, Forgings, Stampings etc. to be ready for Machine Shop by 2-4-25

facilities in the country. 'A' Shop was where all the components manufactured elsewhere on the 323-acre site were brought together for the final assembly of locomotives. The New Work programme sheet reproduced here lists all the component parts of a '56xx' locomotive of Lot No 228, built in 1925. Parts for this engine came from 12 other individual workshops, including the Boiler Shop, the Iron Foundry, the Brass Shop, the Steam Hammer Shop and the Tank Shop.

The process of constructing an engine or group of engines required planning and co-ordination to ensure that the required parts arrived in 'A' Shop at the correct time. The task of building a Great Western engine was not something to be rushed, and a large passenger locomotive like a 'Castle' 4-6-0 could take almost three months to complete. Despite this, at its zenith in the 1930s the Company boasted in its publicity that it was turning out two engines per week. Construction of the fourth batch of five '56xx' locomotives mentioned earlier began on 10 November 1924 and was completed on 23 January 1925.

The workshop was divided by a number of traversers — large, powered rail platforms that allowed locomotives to be moved around the building. On either side were bays where engines — either new or in for repair — were built on an assembly-line basis. Tony Millard, who worked in 'A' Shop both during and after his apprenticeship, remembered that his move to the workshop was made more complicated by the fact that he and the Head Foreman shared the same surname. Summoned to the latter's office on his first morning, he learned from a brief discussion that they were not in fact even distantly related — not that it would have made any difference, as the foreman made it quite clear that there would be 'no favouritism' as far as he was concerned!

The assembly line began with the 'frame gang', who assembled the main locomotive frames. It was vitally important that these be accurately and correctly laid out, and special Zeiss optical equipment was used to ensure correct alignment. Once this had been done, the locomotive cylinders were fitted, the heavy finished castings being positioned by crane and then drilled and bolted into the correct place. As well as the traversers, the men on each gang had the use of two large cranes, each capable of lifting up to 100 tons; these came into play at the next stage, when the locomotive boiler, having been prepared in the 'V' Boiler and 'P1' Boiler Fitting shops, was lowered into position between the engine frames.

The process then moved to what was known as the 'finishing-off' gang; Tony Millard remembered that this was under the leadership of Stan Lewington, a strict and hard taskmaster nicknamed 'The Yellow Peril'. A particularly delicate and dramatic operation was the wheeling of the engine; the entire partially assembled engine was lifted by one of the 100-ton cranes about 8ft in the air, while its driving wheels, already fitted with their bearings, were moved into position on the tracks below using long 'pinch bars' to lever them to approximately where they were needed. As the crane slowly lowered the whole assembly, a man was positioned on each bearing to ensure that it slipped correctly into the engine's horn blocks. In his reminiscences of life in the works, Ken Gibbs recalled: 'It was quite an experience to stand in the pit whilst a frame, complete with boiler, was lowered above you.'[9] Teamwork was required to complete the task safely, communication between the chargehand, the crane-driver and the men on each wheel being vital.

Assembling the frames of a BR Standard Class 4 in 'A' Shop at Swindon in May 1951.

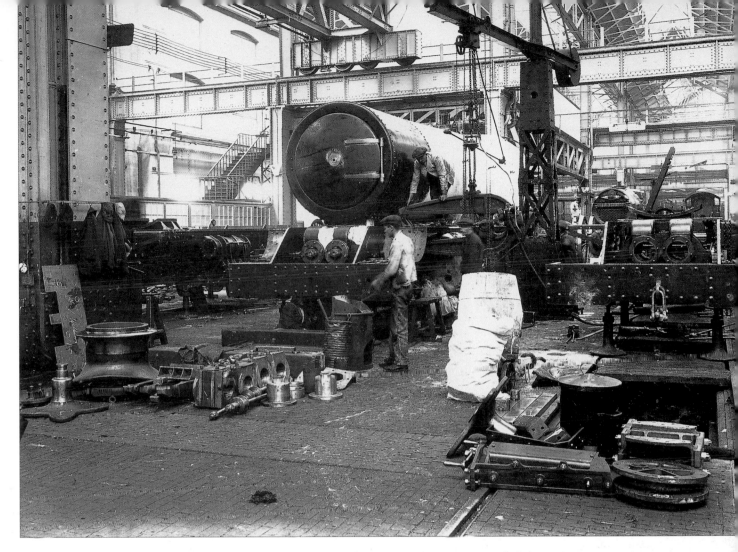

'A' Shop, showing the construction of perhaps the most famous GWR locomotive of all, No 6000 *King George V*, in 1927. Note the asbestos cladding the locomotive's boiler.

Methodically the gang then added other component parts, including the valve-gear and inside motion, connecting rods, brake gear, cab fittings and sanding gear. The same kind of teamwork demonstrated during the wheeling of the engine had to be much in evidence when lifting into position large components such as connecting rods. Ken Gibbs described the process as requiring not only accuracy, whereby all the wheel crank pins were placed in the correct alignment, but also brute strength as perhaps six or seven staff lifted what might be a 10ft steel connecting rod and then stepped forward to manhandle it over the crank pins.

While this work was being carried out, other workmen were cladding the boiler with white asbestos. Although the asbestos was plastered on wet, it flaked or chipped easily when dry, and Tony Millard remembered being showered with asbestos dust when working in the pit under the engine. It would not be until many years later that the

potentially lethal effects of asbestos would be recognised, and many ex-railway staff from the workshops and elsewhere have succumbed to asbestosis, known locally as the 'Swindon disease'.

Once the asbestos had dried, the steel boiler cladding was added, whereupon the locomotive really began to take shape. The process was almost complete when the painters arrived to transform the engine by applying the primer and then the familiar Brunswick (or 'middle chrome') green; unlike some railway works, Swindon had no separate paint shop, so this skilled task was undertaken in the middle of the busy Erecting Shop. One of the last tasks was the addition of a wooden floor for the locomotive cab, done by a carpenter, before the final touch — the brass name- and numberplates. With these in place the locomotive had a final inspection to ensure that all fixtures were secure and that every oiling point had been checked. The engine could then be

One of the 'A' Shop gangs. The only member of staff identified is Mr Fred Kibblewhite, standing on the running plate, second from left. The picture probably dates from the late 1920s. *Ian & Jane Hill*

moved out of the Erecting Shop to the works weighbridge, where the springs were adjusted and tensioned before going on trial. All those who worked in 'A' Shop described this moment as being one of the proudest in their careers; seeing a completed engine on which they had worked from basic components was for some an emotional experience.

It was a tradition that the gang that had worked on an engine were expected to travel on it when it made its first trial run. Once ready, it ran tender-first (again according to tradition) along the Great Western main line down Dauntsey Bank to Chippenham. Since travelling tender-first meant that the crew and any other passengers in the cab would usually end up covered in coal dust, it was another tradition that the gang would sit at the front of the engine, hanging on for dear life to the smokebox handrails. The return trip, usually taken at very high speed, is described by many retired railway staff as one of the most frightening experiences of their career. Going on trial did have a serious side, however, enabling staff to ensure that the engine had no faults, and any minor leaks from pipes or gaskets could be repaired before the engine was sent out to its allocated shed.

Alongside the more glamorous task of building new engines, the day-to-day repair of locomotives continued unabated. Apart from the various gangs already mentioned, the most unpopular place to work in 'A' Shop was in the Stripping Gang. It was the job of staff there to dismantle locomotives brought into the works; being in for repair, these were naturally filthy dirty. Although grease and oil were a hazard, staff that worked on this gang will readily testify that it was the sticky soot which was the biggest problem. Overalls were firmly buttoned up, and string used to seal sleeves and trouser legs, but even this could not prevent soot getting everywhere. As Tony Millard remembers, conditions were worst for men working inside the smokebox or under the locomotive, as every hammer blow dislodged soot and scale that would rain down on those unfortunate enough to be below.

Staff employed in the Carriage & Wagon Works enjoyed an environment very different from that endured by the 'A' Shop Stripping Gang. In 1935 Arthur Webb, whose exploits as an office boy were described earlier, was offered an apprenticeship as a coach-finisher. As was the case elsewhere in the works, he was assigned to a gang and worked with an older man who showed him the ropes. The job of coach-finisher was to make and fit the upholstery in carriages. New work, done in the workshop itself, was always regarded as the most interesting and was also the cleanest; on repairs, dust raised from the old horsehair used to fill the seat cushions was very unpleasant, blackening the ears and noses of workers, who wore old shirt sleeves over their overalls to try to combat the constant rubbing against the moquette seat fabric. Repairs were often effected *in situ* out in the yard, and Arthur Webb recalled that, as the carriages were unheated, this could be extremely cold work in winter. One further job done by the coach-trimmers was to lay carpet and linoleum on the floors between the seats; once again, in the depths of winter this was not the best job: the cold weather not only affected the workmen but also meant that the linoleum was brittle when rolled out. Repairs were also done 'out station' — another Swindon tradition, whereby staff from the workshops were sent to outlying depots to do work without bringing rolling stock back to the factory. Arthur Webb often visited the large carriage sheds at Old Oak Common, as well as carrying out the more unusual task of laying the linoleum at Sudbrook Pumping Station, which served the Severn Tunnel.

Above:
Staff at work maintaining carriages, close to the workshop. The Carriage & Wagon Works complex was to the east of the Gloucester branch.

Right:
The Polishing Shop at Swindon Carriage Works, decorated for the Coronation in May 1937.

Strictly speaking, what went on outside the walls of the great works is beyond the scope of this book, which deals largely with staff in their working lives. However, one feature of life within the railway community at Swindon which does merit attention is that of the annual 'Trip' holiday. Similar in concept to the 'Wakes Week' holidays given to staff in northern mill towns, 'Trip' holiday, usually held in the first week of July, was the highlight of the year for Swindon staff and their families, being the chance to escape the smoky confines of factory life. The first 'Trip' was just that — a day excursion to Oxford, run by the Great Western for its workers in 1847. By the early 20th century, however, the holiday had become 'Trip Week'. At this time the holiday was unpaid, and careful planning (and not a little financial hardship after the event) was required to ensure that a good time was had by all. After World War 2 the holiday became 'Trip Fortnight', having been suspended for the duration of hostilities.

Although there was no holiday pay, the Company did provide free rail tickets for staff and their families to travel to destinations both on the Great Western network and beyond. In June each year staff were asked to make their requests for tickets to management. Officers of the Company did the planning of the special 'Trip' train timetable with Great Western precision, however; this was a major task, as in the early 20th century over 25,000 people were carried on these trains. On 'Trip' morning, special trains left not from Swindon Junction station but from the Carriage Works sidings nearby, as the sheer number of trains would have interfered with the station's normal business. The most popular destinations were Weymouth and Weston-super-Mare, the former being nicknamed 'Swindon by the Sea'! Many retired staff remember the excitement and anticipation generated by 'Trip', although they recall too that going to the same resort each year had its down side; having arrived at Weymouth with one's family, seeing one's workmates at each turn was not always a recipe for a relaxing break! For the more adventurous, 'Interchange tickets' valid on other railways meant that holidays could be taken in more far-flung locations, such as Scotland or North Wales. Most families, however, could afford only a few days away in a boarding house at a location nearer to home, like Weymouth.

The impact of the 'Trip' was felt far beyond the walls of the works, and local shops advertised offers for trippers in advance of the holiday. Townspeople not directly employed by the Great Western at the works in Swindon often had little option but to take a holiday at the same time; with so many of their customers away, shops and other businesses cut their losses and closed too. As one railwayman observed, it was so quiet in the town that 'you could have shot a gun up Regent Street and not hit anyone'!

A view of the Carriage & Wagon Works, where Arthur Webb worked. In the background is the works gas plant, the furthest extent of the site in that direction.

At War

Most of the retired railway staff whose memories have featured in this book began their career just before or during World War 2. It is therefore fitting that a separate section of the book should record some of the unique and sterling work done by Great Western staff during that difficult period. Furthermore, the events of the 1939-45 conflict would change many of the working practices and attitudes prevalent before the war, with the nationalisation of Britain's railways in 1948 bringing the history of the Great Western Railway as an independent company to an end. Indeed, one of the most significant developments at the outbreak of war in 1939 was that all the 'Big Four' companies and London Transport were effectively nationalised anyway under the auspices of the Railway Executive, placing the railways under the control of the Government.

For most staff, on a day-to-day basis little changed initially, with 'business as usual' being the order of the day. The Company made little comment about the new arrangement, although the General Manager did write to staff warning them that effort would be required 'in the strenuous and difficult days ahead'. Little did many staff know that during the next five years they would experience the perils of the Blackout and

A symbolic image of a female member of staff pasting a famous wartime poster at Paddington station.

bombing, shortages, long hours and many other trials.

Although Great Western staff had played a key role in the huge operation to evacuate school children from Paddington to the country in the days immediately after the declaration of war on Germany in September 1939, the impact of the war did not sink in with many staff during the first few months of what became known as the 'Phoney War'. However, the Blackout imposed to counter the threat of German air raids was compounded by atrocious weather, which made the operation of the railway all the more difficult. Cold and foggy weather over the Christmas period was followed in the early part of 1940 by what was described as perhaps the worst weather for a century. Ice and heavy falls of snow brought the Great Western network to a virtual standstill, with almost 500 miles of signal and telegraph cables being brought down.

Ernie Ross described how much of the damage occurred one weekend, when, after a Sunday of solid rain which had saturated everything, there was a sudden frost, which meant that the millions of water droplets turned to ice. That night all that could be heard was the 'crashing of tree branches overloaded with tons of ice'.[1] Not only did many of the branches crash onto the track or

117

onto telegraph wires; the wires themselves also snapped under the weight of the ice. Ross was working at Devizes station and, arriving for work at 6am, soon realised that all was not well. The ice had made it impossible for the electric token system to work between the signalboxes at Devizes and Seend, further down the line, and he was forced to make a perilous journey by ganger's trolley to the intermediate 'box at Bromham before walking on to Seend to exchange Pilot Working forms, which replaced the token system in situations like this. He remembered slipping and falling many times, as 'there was no safe footing anywhere'.[2]

Communication was difficult for almost three days,

Above:
GWR staff loading the components for Anderson shelters in 1939.

Left:
This snowy image was in fact taken in the winter of 1947, but it illustrates the problems faced by the Company in the first winter of the war.

compounded by the fact that many signal wires were frozen solid, meaning that trains had to be signalled by hand with staff using flags, as the semaphore signals could not be operated. Knowledge of the rules and regulations, concentration and patience were all necessary to allow trains to run safely in such difficult circumstances. Despite the long delays suffered by passenger and goods trains, few accidents were reported. However, the toll on staff was high, and reports after the event noted that sickness levels were up by as much as a quarter.

It was not until the spring of 1940 that there was a realisation amongst staff that the war was anything but phoney. Germany's invasion of the Low Countries on 10 May and the subsequent retreat of the British Expeditionary Force back to the Channel ports brought the Great Western firmly onto a war footing, both on land and at sea. The story of the Dunkirk evacuation and the role played by Great Western ships has been told a number of times in some detail.[3] Under fire from enemy bombing and shelling, staff showed exceptional bravery and dedication, rescuing thousands of British and French troops from the beaches and harbour. The achievement is all the more amazing when one considers that the crews of such ships were normally employed on the relatively peaceful job of running services like those operated by the Company from Weymouth to Jersey. Military authorities had considered putting naval commanders and crew onto the ships, but, when asked, the master of the SS *St Helier* is reported to have said: 'Not on your life you won't!'

Back on dry land in England, the staff of the Great Western had another important role to play in the aftermath of the Dunkirk operation. Although most of the Channel ports were in areas served by the Southern Railway, the GWR still bore the brunt of many of the troop-train movements, which were generated in the days and weeks after the evacuation. Records show that the operation involved transporting by rail no fewer than 319,116 officers and men, of whom 182,808 were carried by the Great Western on more than 800 special military trains. To permit

GREAT WESTERN RAILWAY

Notice to Passengers

Passengers are advised to take shelter during an Air Raid and not to remain on the station platforms, where there may be a serious risk of danger from falling glass and splinters.

August, 1940.

J. MILNE,
General Manager.

Stations were dangerous places to be, especially those with large overall glass roofs, as this poster makes clear to passengers.

this, many normal services were cancelled, and timetables subject to drastic alteration.

Ernie Ross remembered being woken after midnight by a policeman, who instructed him to go to the station immediately and unlock the premises. Arriving at the station he was greeted by three army officers, who, having sworn him and his staff to secrecy, informed them of the dreadful news from Dunkirk. They were then told to expect, in the next few hours, trainloads of men evacuated from the beaches; Devizes had both a regimental headquarters and a large training camp nearby and was close to other large military bases in Wiltshire. When trains arrived, the exhausted men were moved as quickly as possible into waiting lorries. Ernie and his staff were confronted with a disturbing sight: the evacuated men were so tired that some were impossible to rouse or collapsed on the road while waiting to board their transport. Uneaten food littered the inside of the trains, the men being too tired to eat it. In all, six trains were unloaded at the station, and although the station staff were tired, Ernie Ross noted that 'the men we were working for were in far worse plight, and the army brewed gallons of tea and there was plenty to eat'.[4] The scene was repeated all over the Great Western network, and, along with station staff and signalmen, footplatemen and guards worked long hours to bring the operation to a successful conclusion. Writing in the July 1940 *Great Western Railway Magazine*, Company Chairman Viscount Horne thanked staff for their efforts, claiming that the story of the work done in June 1940 by GWR employees was 'one that could be read with the greatest pride by all our staff'.

With the German army seemingly poised to invade Britain, tension was high during the summer of 1940, and the beginning of the Battle of Britain on 2 August heralded a new phase of the war. All staff had been trained in Air Raid Precautions, circulars and other booklets having been issued by the Company as early as 1938, but many staff readily admitted that during the early part of the war they had become rather complacent. They were jolted into action

The scene at Newton Abbot station in 1940, after the first serious raid on GWR property. *Great Western Trust*

when, on 20 August, 14 people were killed and another 29 seriously injured when three aircraft attacked the GWR station at Newton Abbot. This was merely a prelude to what became known as 'The Blitz' — a sustained bombing campaign that would continue through much of 1941. During this time Great Western trains, staff and premises would suffer greatly in an onslaught that would cause huge disruption to the network but ultimately not disable it.

The fact that the 'Year of the Blitz' did not result in the total destruction of the Great Western network was in no small part due to the resourcefulness and bravery of its staff. At the height of the Blitz, staff at stations such as Paddington, Bristol, Birmingham and Plymouth bore the brunt of heavy raids, with both damage and casualties being sustained in the process. Matters were no better in South Wales, where the extensive dock facilities owned by the Great Western also came under attack. A graphic illustration of how these raids affected staff is provided by the recollections of Bill Morgan, who, as a fireman based at Neyland in West Wales, worked trains all over South Wales during the war.

On one particular evening in February 1941, Bill and his colleague Ted Rees were due to book on at Landore shed before heading light-engine to Swansea to take over a down parcels train from Paddington at just after midnight. The

warning sirens had sounded late that afternoon, and Bill described seeing waves of aircraft dropping flares and incendiaries on Swansea and Landore, followed by bombs which were still dropping when they left the lodging house to go to work. It was at this point that they regretted not having the tin helmets with which they had been issued early in the war — an example of the casual attitude that had prevailed until the onset of the Blitz. Bill's was hanging on the back of the kitchen door at home, and his mate's had been lost on an engine some months earlier!

Landore station seemed to be unscathed, and, having booked on duty, Bill and Ted made their way cautiously down to Swansea. The raid was so heavy that they did not bother to use the canvas anti-glare screens, used to hide the glow of the firebox from enemy aircraft, as they inched slowly in to Swansea station. Despite the ferocity of the raid, the connecting service arrived on time, much to their relief; feeling like 'sitting ducks', they were keen to get away from the station as soon as they could and head for the relative safety of the countryside (and, eventually, Neyland). At this point, however, things ceased to go to plan. No sooner had Bill got underneath the locomotive to couple it up to the parcels train than 'it sounded as if all hell was let loose'[5]; the remains of the glass platform canopy crashed down, and he flung himself under the tender as 'twisted steel supports collapsed along the platform'. All hell had indeed broken loose, and utter confusion reigned, with debris flying around; the crew took cover under the locomotive, staying there for over an hour and a quarter whilst the raid raged above them. Before diving for cover, Bill had noticed that all the signals were at Danger, preventing any of the trains from escaping the inferno. This was an established procedure, although a GWR circular issued in October 1939 instructed that, if it were deemed safe to do so, a signalman or station-master could instruct a driver to proceed at a speed not exceeding 15mph.[6] Clearly, whilst the air raid was at its height no one at Swansea station felt that this was the case!

At 4am, during a lull in the bombing, Bill and Ted were stirred by a guard's whistle and climbed back up onto the platform to await the 'right away', which, to their relief, they received within a few minutes. Pulling out of the station, they noticed staff and emergency workers running for cover yet again, as another wave of bombers approached the city. Although Bill did not give the date of this incident, it almost certainly took place on the night of 19 February 1941; Company records reveal that, besides the damage caused to Platform 4 of Swansea High Street station, the tug *Carnforth* was sunk by bombs falling on the nearby docks. On the following two nights the station suffered further, three staff being injured, and the ARP Control Office, the Refreshment Rooms, the District Goods Office and the station's own Goods Office being badly damaged, while on each occasion water, gas and electricity supplies were disrupted for some hours.

Pulling away from the station, Bill and Ted began to feel safer, but this lasted only as far as Llanelli, the next stop, for here too an air raid was in full swing. Bill remembered: 'It was like going back into a trap again. Bells were ringing, whistles blowing, shouts, confusion and chaos greeted us as we slowed to a halt at the platform.' He confessed that, as they headed deeper into the Carmarthenshire countryside, away from the industrial valleys, he felt almost guilty at being safe; all they could now see was an ominous orange glow in the eastern sky. Arriving back at Neyland at 8.45 in the morning, he was both tired and relieved to be home.

Returning to Swansea the following day, Bill was stunned to see the devastation wrought by the air raids, with 'entire streets disappeared in a mass of rubble'. The damaged lines in and out of Swansea were nevertheless a hive of activity, with permanent-way men and engineers checking the track; throughout the war, Great Western staff were able to restore damaged trackwork at almost miraculous speed after raids, enabling at least some trains to be operated within hours, so that the network was never truly paralysed, however bad the bomb damage.

The mental and physical strains of being under attack during an air raid were not the only perils facing footplate staff in the war; perhaps the biggest fear was of direct attack from individual enemy aircraft, particularly at night. A steam locomotive running across a blacked-out landscape was difficult to hide, the glare emitted from the firebox being the most difficult to obscure, and a 1939 circular issued to staff urged that 'every precaution must be taken during firing to prevent firebox glow at all times during the hours of darkness'.[7] The solution was to fit every locomotive with the 'anti-glare screens' mentioned earlier. These were canvas tarpaulins that could be stretched across from the locomotive cab to the tender. Initially it was thought that around seven different variations of the design would be necessary to cover all the different engines owned by the Great Western, but this estimate turned out to be very optimistic, and eventually the Drawing Office at Swindon listed no fewer than 45 different sheets, each with a different arrangement of bolts and hooks! Arthur Webb, whose career in the Carriage & Wagon Works at Swindon was outlined in Chapter 5, described working on these screens while still an apprentice coach-trimmer in 1939. The job was given 'top priority' over his normal day-to-day work, and he remembered laying out the canvas between the tracks in the yard behind his workshop rather than doing the work inside. The canvas was painted black and then cut into lengths and sewn together, with eyelets inserted according to the class of engine.

Although reasonably effective in reducing locomotives' visibility to enemy aircraft, the screens — known as 'sails' by footplate staff — were not popular. In warm and humid weather they made life on the footplate unbearably hot — and damp, as condensation ran down the inside of the canvas. Matters were made worse by the fact that, on the outbreak of war, the glass side windows were painted over and, later (as locomotives came in for overhaul), were properly plated over with steel, further restricting the already limited view of signals.

The memories of Gordon Shurmer, based at Swindon locomotive shed, give an idea of the conditions endured by footplate staff in wartime. In 1939 Gordon had volunteered for active duty in the forces and had actually got as far as attending a medical in Bath; however, within 10 days of his doing so, railway work was designated a 'reserved occupation', with the result that at this stage in the war, other than in exceptional circumstances, staff could not be called up. Given the need for extra troop trains even early in the war, this was a wise decision but one borne out of the experience of the Great War, when railway companies had found it increasingly difficult to run the service required of them by the Government once so many of their staff had volunteered or been conscripted into the Forces.

Two views of the air-raid precautions adopted by locomotive crews. The protective anti-glare sheeting can be seen on top of the cab of No 6011 *King James I*, whilst the plated-over window is also apparent in the picture of No 5020 *Trematon Castle*.

In 1940, to combat the shortage of footplate staff, the Great Western suspended the compulsory retirement of staff at 60 years of age. Those attaining this age during that year were told they could remain in service until the age of 61 or the end of hostilities. If they did not wish to continue working, staff could apply in writing to the Divisional Superintendent, but the implication in the announcement was that most (if fit) were expected to 'carry on'.

The extra trains run during the war period obviously required extra crews, and, as we discovered earlier in this volume, in our survey of life on the footplate, war did accelerate the sometimes agonisingly slow progress of footplate staff through the links by seniority. Gordon remembered that he spent relatively short periods as a fireman in shunting and goods links at Swindon before moving up to firing passenger trains — a situation which would not have prevailed prewar. Perhaps to allay fears that cleaners were being promoted through the grades too quickly, Chief Mechanical Engineer F. W. Hawksworth wrote to his senior staff in May 1941, warning them that no cleaner, regardless of age, should be allowed to take up temporary firing duties unless he had been in the Company's service for at least three months.[8]

If steam locomotives were an obvious target at night due to the glare from their fireboxes, they could be just as vulnerable during daylight hours. German fighters and bombers with no specific target would often find a railway line and then follow its route until they found a train that they could attack. One particular incident which Gordon Shurmer still remembers with some trepidation occurred one day when he was firing a freight train on Dauntsey Bank, near Swindon. It was the fireman's duty to look out from the footplate to check on the train, and on this occasion, as Gordon was crossing the cab and looking back down the line of wagons, he saw, to his horror, flying just above the level of the wagons, in broad daylight, a German aircraft! Like many young men of his generation during World War 2, he knew a bit about German 'planes, and the briefest look had told him that this was a Heinkel He111 bomber. It drew level with the locomotive and was so close that Gordon could see the cross on its fuselage and swastika on its tail; to make things worse, the pilot even had the temerity to wave at Gordon as he banked his 'plane away

Above:
The remains of GWR 0-6-0PT
No 1729 after an attack at
Castle Cary in 1942.
Little wonder that footplate
crew like Gordon Shurmer
were so worried about being
attacked by enemy planes!

Right:
The effect of German machine
guns on a GWR locomotive
in the Newton Abbot raid.
A similar effect was achieved
in the incident described by
Ernie Ross near Weymouth.

from the train and climbed out of sight! The terrified locomotive crew knew that it was highly likely that the aircraft would return to attack the locomotive broadside-on, with disastrous results; Gordon and his driver knew all about 'train-busting' techniques, which the Allies had themselves practised in France, to devastating effect. For some reason, however, the 'plane did not return, whether due to lack of ammunition or fuel, and the crew lived to fight another day. Gordon has another theory — that the pilot's father was an engine-driver. In any event, as Gordon says, they didn't need to take a laxative for a fortnight!

Ernie Ross recounted another 'close shave' in his book *Tales of the Rails*. Working at Yeovil station, he described the arrival of a Great Western '63xx' 2-6-0 tender locomotive on a service from Weymouth. The station shunter went to speak to the driver, who told him that a German aircraft had

been tracking his train. The line north of Weymouth was well known to footplate staff as a familiar haunt of enemy aircraft at a loose end after attacking targets at the naval base at Portland. The driver thought that one of the coaches had been hit by the fighter, and the attack had forced them to pause in Grinscone Tunnel until the raider had run low on fuel. When the driver had calmed down, the shunter told him that it might be worth taking water at the station, but the driver disagreed. 'What for? We can get to Westbury easily with this engine.'[9] The shunter then pointed out the neat, straight line of bullet holes along the side of the tender, from which water was leaking profusely. The shocked crew, now more than ever aware of their narrow escape, duly went about plugging the holes with corks and rags before taking more water from the crane at the end of the platform.

Footplate staff were nervous enough when bringing trains

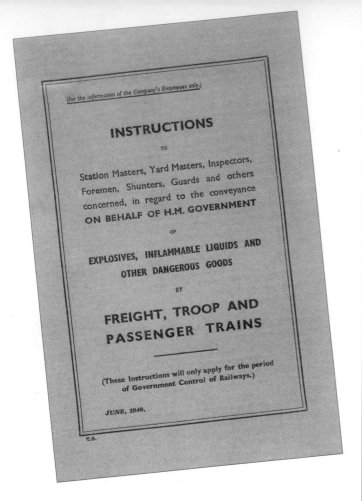

Special instructions for the running of ammunition trains and petrol trains, issued in 1940.

through routes such as that described above; they were even more jumpy when the trains contained particularly hazardous loads — specifically ammunition, petrol or aviation fuel. There was more than enough danger to contend with in peacetime, the risk being that sparks from the locomotive chimney might ignite the load behind them. The rules and regulations stipulated that no more than five explosives wagons should be marshalled in any train, but in time of war this was clearly not realistic, and the rule was relaxed to allow up to 60 wagons to be coupled together. Even so, trains of this type were not allowed to run through the Severn Tunnel or to pass other trains in other tunnels. Train speeds were also limited to 40mph, which could be a mixed blessing; locomotive crews felt that, given this limit, it was hard to outrun any aircraft chasing a train with such a dangerous load! In the case of fuel trains, to try to camouflage petrol-tank wagons against air attack, from July 1940 the Company painted them battleship grey. The completion of a number of pipelines from the South Wales docks to the South Coast reduced the requirement for such trains and thus the risk to

locomotive crews. However, in the months leading up to the Allied invasion of Europe, millions of gallons of aviation fuel were needed by Allied bombers softening up targets in France, so regular fuel trains were reintroduced.

As the war progressed locomotive crews found themselves working more and more on special trains, including those just described as well as many others carrying tanks and other military equipment. In the run-up to D-Day in 1944 additional strain was put on the railway by the vastly increased numbers of troop trains bringing soldiers from ports to bases and transit camps close to the South Coast. Just how much this traffic increased may be gleaned from the fact that in 1941 the number of troop trains run by the Great Western averaged 400 per month; the following year the figure was broadly the same, but in 1943 the monthly figures increased steadily, and in November 1,043 trains were run. In the six months up to D-Day itself nearly 6,500 troop trains were run by the Company; when the additional number of munitions and equipment trains is included the total rises to a staggering 18,609 trains worked between January and July 1944. Little wonder, then, that footplate crew and guards were pushed to their very limits during this crucial period.

Large numbers of the troops moved before D-Day were from the United States. Many had disembarked from ships that had arrived in South Wales docks owned by the Great Western, and, as the invasion approached, they were moved from bases all over the West Country to camps nearer the South Coast. Gordon Shurmer recalls a rather sobering experience whilst working an American troop train. The soldiers had begun their journey at the Old Town station at Swindon, on the old Midland & South Western Junction Railway route, which ran south from Swindon to the coast via Marlborough and Andover. Arriving at the southern terminus of the route at Southampton, the soldiers de-trained at the station, and Gordon left his engine to begin the regular task of walking through the train and picking up items left by the 'Yanks'. Compared with British soldiers on relatively meagre rations, the Americans were profligate, to say the least, leaving, as Gordon says, 'everything but their rifles' on the train. An alert traincrew could acquire all manner of goodies, picking up comics, candies and fruit. On this occasion the guard was making his way from the other end of the train, and when he and Gordon met up, they would share the spoils. Walking back up the platform however, Gordon could not help but notice that all was not well; the troops, in a rebellious mood, had thrown their rifles off the platform into the ballast and were refusing to move. As Gordon reached the locomotive cab he saw an American lieutenant pick out three of his men and frogmarch them up the platform towards the engine. He lined them up against

A '45xx' 2-6-2 tank locomotive (No 5534) on a wartime munitions train.
On this occasion the load comprised Allied tanks.

the locomotive, pointed his machine gun at them and told the rest that he would 'drop' these three unless order was restored. Quickly the remaining troops jumped off the platform and grabbed their rifles before being marched off to an uncertain fate! What had promised to be a straightforward duty for the crew that day had turned out rather differently, and Gordon remembers that his driver was 'white as a sheet'!

Goods and passenger guards whose task it was to look after the train shared the stresses and strains suffered by footplate staff. For the goods guards it was particularly tough, since they could not leave their train until relieved. Services were often delayed by air raids, especially when major centres were under attack, and, as a result, scores of trains could be stuck in loops and sidings waiting for the 'All Clear' to be sounded. The guard stayed with the train, often stuck in his brake van for many hours in the Blackout; as many staff would recount, it could be a lonely job! During these long shifts, which in the worst cases could last up to 18 hours, the guards and footplate crew worked as a team, sharing what food and tea they had. The relationship was not always a smooth one, however; an accident report dating from May 1942 records that the guard on a service from Treherbert to Cardiff was injured when he was knocked off balance when the driver of 0-6-2 tank locomotive No 5601 applied the

brakes at a home signal near Pontypridd. The train consisted of 60 empty coal wagons, and the driver stated indignantly that although it was 'dark and misty . . . I applied my brakes in the usual manner'.[10] Clearly the 'usual manner' may not have been gentle enough for the poor guard at the back of the long train!

Passenger guards were confronted by a completely different set of problems, albeit also compounded by the wartime conditions. For them it was the Blackout that gave the most trouble. It was the responsibility of the guard to ensure that no light was showing from the carriages in his charge, so during the journey it was his duty to make sure that all the Blackout blinds covering each window were fully pulled down, preventing any escape of light. Given the dimness of the lamps and shades within the carriages, reading passengers' tickets was also extremely awkward.

Potentially the most dangerous situations in the Blackout occurred when trains were approaching stations. In blacked-out conditions, it was extremely difficult for passengers to judge where they were and, indeed, if they had arrived at their own station. Not only could they not see outside; when they did reach a station, the destination or running-in boards giving the location had usually been painted out for security reasons. Many passengers disembarked from their train and watched it disappear into the distance before

A special notice warning passengers about blackout precautions as applied to GWR carriages in 1942.

realising that they were actually in the wrong place! Inconvenient though this may have been, particularly when the next train was some hours away, far more serious were accidents that occurred both on and off trains as a result of the Blackout conditions.

A hand-written report of an accident at Cullompton in Devon, dating from October 1942, clearly demonstrates this.[11] A Royal Naval nurse, Miss Webber Hillcrest, suffered a broken leg when she fell from the 8.10pm Exeter–Taunton service; Acting Passenger Guard H. Gardner reported that the injured passenger had been told at Exeter that Tiverton Junction was the fifth stop. This may well have been the case, but the train was held at the home signal outside the station, and Miss Hillcrest, thinking that the train had arrived in the station, stepped out into the darkness and fell onto the ballast. When the train had come to a halt, the unfortunate guard had tried in vain to warn passengers not to leave the train when he saw a number of doors opening. The locomotive crew and a local policeman rendered first aid at the scene, but hospital treatment at Tiverton was necessary for the injured and presumably shocked passenger.

A similar incident, involving a local train from Birmingham Snow Hill, occurred in January 1942 at Olton; the train drew into the station, but for some reason, the last two coaches were not level with the platform. To make matters worse, the hapless guard on duty on the train did not realise the danger until too late, allowing a number of passengers to fall out onto the track. If this were not bad enough, he compounded matters by failing to notice at least three of these passengers lying on the ground, being too busy shouting at those on the train to 'shut the doors'. One of the passengers, a Mr Farncombe, was forced to clamber up onto the platform and get help from the stationmaster on the other side of the footbridge. No doubt the guard received a stiff reprimand from both the stationmaster and his supervisor, although the incident serves to illustrate the perils of travelling in the Blackout!

Violet Lee was born in 1923 into a railway family, her father being employed as a foreman shunter and later a platform inspector for the Great Western. In 1940 her father asked if she would like to become a passenger guard, and after two interviews, the second with the stationmaster at Gloucester, she joined the GWR, although, as she noted in an account of her career written in 1990,[12] it was made very clear to her that this was a 'wartime appointment only' and that, when men returned from the war, she would be expected to resign from her job. Following a brief spell of training, Violet began working one of three shifts — alternately 5.30am–1pm, 11am–3pm and 2pm–10pm — with one Sunday off in every three weeks. In all she worked as a guard for seven years, with a brief break when she fell pregnant after two years. Tragically her husband died of war wounds at just 22, and she had little choice but to return to work, a supportive family looking after her son whilst she was away. She began her day by checking in with the driver and fireman before walking to the end of the train to ensure that the tail lamp was present and lit. The weight, number and description of each coach was then entered in her logbook, and the emergency chains in each carriage checked. After reporting the weight of the train to the driver, she ensured all doors were closed, and, with a blast of a whistle from the stationmaster or platform inspector and a wave of her green flag, the train would be off.

Dealing with the ever-present problems of the Blackout was an integral part of the guard's job; as well as all the checks already mentioned, Violet would walk along the platform shouting 'Mind the blinds please! Pull the blinds please!' The troop trains described earlier, particularly those packed with American servicemen, were a source of luxuries such as cigarettes, chocolate, sugar and occasionally a pair of nylon stockings! Violet recalled that her son did not know what a lemon looked like until she was given two

Left:
Platform staff at Gloucester in 1944. Violet Lee, who contributed her memories to this book, is second from the right. *Violet Lee collection*

Below:
Shunting in blackout conditions during World War 2 was even more perilous than in peacetime, as this atmospheric picture shows.

by a sailor returning on leave. One dark Friday night she collected a classified document on the Hereford–Aldermaston service and delivered it at Gloucester for onward passage. More worrying was the sight of Prisoner of War trains with 'blinds drawn', stabled in the centre road at Gloucester station. In her seven-year stint as a passenger guard she travelled widely on local services in the Stroud Valley and on the Cheltenham–Honeybourne route and on branch-line services in the Forest of Dean. The local farming communities in such areas were a good source of food to augment meagre wartime rations; eggs, rabbits, honey, chicken, bacon and vegetables and the famous Blaisdon Red plums were all gratefully received! Violet confirmed the comradeship felt by many railway staff, despite the sometimes difficult conditions under which they worked, recalling that she 'was always treated with the greatest of respect by passengers and all the people I met' and adding that 'I met people from all walks of life and talked to anyone'

— a sentiment common to many who lived and worked through World War 2.

Away from the front line of railway operation, the effects of the war were felt keenly at Swindon Works. Being such a large and strategically important site, the works was bound to be a key target for enemy bombers. Air Raid Precautions were taken very seriously, and the first and most major task was to ensure that the Blackout was total throughout the great site. The biggest job by far was the painting of the huge expanses of glass in the rooflights of most of the workshops, plunging them into an artificially lit gloom that was to last for most of the war. Staff employed in the works at the time remember that working under electric or gas lighting was hard on the eyes and to some extent disorientating, especially when they were working on the night shift. The hooters which summoned men to work in peacetime were silenced and used only to sound air-raid warnings, for which purpose they were powerful enough to serve the whole town.

Additional air-raid shelters had to be provided at Swindon Works to accommodate the 12,000 or so staff — a considerable task. The cost of these alone exceeded £23,000, and further money had to be spent on gas-decontamination centres around the site. Swindon staff were asked to volunteer for ARP and Fire Watching duties when they were not working; with such a vast site it was necessary to have large numbers of staff available day and night. John Fleetwood recalls being part of the Fire Watching detail. The area he usually patrolled when on duty was known as the Concentration Yard — a large timber yard covering about five acres situated at the west end of the works site. Stacks of timber up to 30ft high dominated the area. Two old carriages were positioned there to accommodate the Fire Watchers, and looking back, he reflected that, while they were there to look out for the deadly incendiary bombs, it was unlikely that they could have done much to counter the effects of a concentrated air attack, armed as they were only with buckets of water and stirrup pumps! While the younger members of staff on duty dozed in the carriages, some of the 'old-timers', who were also expected to do their bit, disappeared in search of ale, returning after a couple of pints at one of the local pubs which still had beer!

Some of the men working in the Factory had experience of wartime conditions, having been employed during World War 1. With the outbreak of hostilities in 1939 management, particularly Chief Mechanical Engineer C. B. Collett, hoped that on this occasion the GWR would be able to escape the demands of the War Office and Ministry of

The timber yard where John Fleetwood spent many nights fire-watching at Swindon Works.

Swindon did much work in the Great War as well as during the later conflict. This picture shows Inspector Godsell and staff who had assisted in the shipment of Ambulance Trains produced at the works from 1914 to 1916.

Munitions, which over the course of World War 1 had increased to such an extent that the day-to-day output of the workshops had suffered greatly; standards of locomotive and rolling-stock maintenance had fallen markedly, but the Factory had produced shells at the rate of over 2,500 per week, as well as manufacturing naval guns and mountings, ambulance trains and other equipment. Collett was to be disappointed, however; although in 1939 and early 1940 the amount of war work was modest, by 1941 the gravity of the war situation meant that the skills and equipment available at Swindon were increasingly called upon by the War Office.

For the workforce, one of the most obvious changes was the increase in hours worked, as a system of day and night shifts was instituted. John Fleetwood remembered working a pattern of a fortnight on nights, then a fortnight on days; he hated working the night shift, and recalled that his body clock and eating habits took a while to adjust! Not surprisingly, the combination of these shifts and Fire Watching or Home Guard duties frequently took its toll on staff. The annual 'Trip Holiday' was abolished for the duration, not only to allow production to continue but also because many of the beaches and holiday spots visited by Swindon workers and their families were either in Restricted Areas or surrounded by barbed wire or tank traps! Instead, staff holidays were staggered through the year, allowing production to continue unabated.

Tony Millard recalled that during the war, although they worked long hours and could earn good wages, staff had little opportunity to spend those wages, either through tiredness or due to shortages. The overriding impression given by those who worked at Swindon and elsewhere on the railway during the war was that it seemed never-ending — as John Fleetwood said, 'It was a *long* war'. One concession was the relaxation (except in shops where wood or inflammable materials were used) in 1941 of the rule prohibiting smoking in the workshops.

As the war dragged on, and more and more men were conscripted into the armed forces, staff shortages became acute; moreover, matters had not been made any easier by the relocation or 'loan' of some 900 skilled staff from Swindon to other factories and munitions facilities being set up around the country. Many staff in the works tried to enlist, but, as railway work was a Reserved Occupation, this was not easy. John Fleetwood hoped to join the Air Force but was warned that he would not be able to return to complete his apprenticeship after the end of the war. With this in mind he decided to stay and see out his five years in the Foundry.

By 1941 the blanket system of Reserved Occupations had been discontinued and replaced by a more flexible system, whereby the deferment of conscription was judged on an individual and occupational basis. The continuing loss of

Above:
Existing skills were put to good use in war work. This davit for a minesweeper was being machined in 'G' Shop in November 1940.

Left:
Two types of 4,000lb casing produced in 'L2' Shop at Swindon and photographed in 1941.

staff to the forces could be stemmed only by the employment of women, in a repeat of events which had been played out during World War 1, barely 20 years previously. Once again women played a critical role in the war effort, and once again the Great Western was the most reluctant company to recruit women into its service. The reticence of Chief Mechanical Engineer C. B. Collett to involve Swindon in war work has already been mentioned, and this was mirrored by a similar lack of enthusiasm for the employment of women in the works and locomotive depots under his control. Rosa Matheson, in her research on the role of women on the Great Western Railway,[13] has noted that some of the lack of enthusiasm shown by Collett and other senior management may have been due to an acknowledgement that working conditions in the railway factory at Swindon were scarcely adequate for the men already employed there, let alone for the women being brought in. As she writes, Alfred Williams in his book on the Railway Works called it 'dingy, dirty and drab' and 'dark, sombre and repellent'. No matter how poor conditions were, however, the overriding needs of the war effort were paramount.

C. B. Collett retired finally in July 1941, and his successor F. W. Hawksworth began to make some inroads into the increased employment of women, although, judging from some of the surviving correspondence, the task was not an easy one. Some idea of the speed of progress can be gained from a report submitted to the GWR board in March 1941, which revealed that the Great Western had employed just 2,052 women to date, most of whom worked in the Traffic

Above: An Ambulance Train carriage converted by the GWR at Swindon in February 1945. *National Railway Museum*

Below: Women had increasingly been employed in the Railway Works and elsewhere in the system, particularly in the offices. *National Railway Museum*

Left:
A female member of staff working on a Mk. VII two-pounder gun mounting, produced for the Admiralty in 1942.

Right:
The new canteen built in the Carriage & Wagon Works in 1943, which was used for social activities as well as a mess room.

Below right:
A letter regarding the salaries of female clerks, issued in 1942.

Below far right:
A wartime identity card issued to a female member of staff at Didcot.

 GREAT WESTERN RAILWAY.

Telephone:
No. 1530.

SHEET WORKS MANAGER'S OFFICE,
STORES DEPARTMENT,
WORCESTER STATION.

May 12th.,1942.

13 MAY 1942
STORES 1ST
SWINDON

Please quote this reference :—

A

Your reference :—

S/HRW.

Dear Sir,

Women Clerks taking the place of Males.

With reference to yours of March 3rd., I shall be glad
to know whether Mr Webb has had an opportunity of raising this
matter again with the Chief Staff & Establishment Officer.

As indicated in the memo. which accompanied my letter
of Feb.20th last there has been a considerable reduction in the
expense of running the Accounting Section of the Office due to
the release of Male Clerks, and there should be ample scope for
some adjustment to be made in favour of the two female Clerks in
question. Perhaps you will kindly let me hear further from you.

Yours truly,

W.E.Walling

G.F.Boxall Esq.,
Swindon.

No. 66652

GWR
IDENTIFICATION CARD
GREAT WESTERN RAILWAY

The undermentioned person is authorised to
be on the Lines and Premises on the Great
Western Railway Company while in the
execution of his duty. This card is valid until
cancelled or withdrawn.

NAME IN FULL Mrs. B. M. Jones
DEPARTMENT Stores
GRADE Woman Clerk
STATIONED AT DIDCOT
SIGNATURE OF HOLDER B M Jones

This Identification Card must be signed in
ink by the holder immediately he receives it,
and be carried by him until further notice when
engaged in work on the Railway. It must be
produced at any time on request, and the
holder must, if required, sign his name as a
proof of his identity.

Signature of
Issuing Officer

General Manager.

Two views of steam hammers being operated by women. That on the left, dating from 1946, illustrates how tiring the work could be when the handle had to be pulled repeatedly; the second dates from 1942.

Department as porters, ticket-collectors and carriage-cleaners. Hawksworth was forced to write to Divisional Superintendents on a number of occasions, urging them to redouble their efforts. By 1942 the number of women employed had increased to around 8,000, and by the end of the war this total exceeded 16,000, replacing the 15,000 or so men who had been conscripted into the forces.

Most of the women employed at Swindon were directed there by the local Labour Exchange. As Rosa Matheson notes, they did not know what sort of work they would be doing, only whether they were working in the offices or workshops, and no account was taken of whether they were single, married or the mothers of very young children.[14] Others, however, came from much further away; single women with no dependants, from places such as Bristol and the East End of London, where there were surpluses of labour, found themselves mobilised and posted to the grimy workshops at Swindon.

The women at Swindon found themselves doing jobs that in prewar years had been regarded as well beyond their physical capabilities. Interviewed in 1996, Phyllis Saunders described how she began work at Swindon when she was 18. On arrival she was sent to the Blacksmiths' Shop, where she was trained to be a hammer-driver, operating one of the largest hammers in the workshop. She remembered the works as being terrible: 'It was filthy. I thought it was a terrible place to have to work,' she recalled. The physical strain of working in such conditions took its toll; the ash floors gave her blisters (which healed in time), and the repetitive strain of operating the steam hammer made her arms ache. Before working 'inside' she had worked for four years in a tailoring company, which had placed different demands on her, but, as she noted, 'I got used to it and all the aches and pains wore off.'

Violet Joynes began her stint in the works as a welder but quickly moved on to become the first female crane-driver in the Factory. Operating one of the overhead cranes in the 'L2' Tank Shop, she lifted locomotive tenders and side tanks around the workshops until it was discovered that she was only 18 years old. Union regulations decreed that only those over 21 could operate cranes, so she was sent into the Tool Room, 'milling, drilling, grinding, turning'. Her railwayman father had taught her all he knew about tools, which was a great help, and when work dried up she moved to the 'R' Machine Shop, where she not only operated turning machines but also ended up setting other people's machines, for which she was paid a shilling extra in her basic pay. Amazingly, as a labourer on piecework, Violet Joynes remembered being paid £14 per week — a good wage for the time, and more than that earned by her father, a tradesman. Because of the ill-feeling this caused, she stopped showing her father her paypacket; 'then he didn't know how much I earned'.

When she was almost 21, Violet was asked to go to the 'V' Boiler Shop as a crane-driver. Here the cranes were larger and more powerful than in 'L2' Shop, and, instead of lifting tenders and tanks, she was in charge of larger and far heavier locomotive boilers. Little if any training was given, and, as she was already considered a crane-driver, no one told her that moving boilers was quite a different operation. On her first job, that of turning a boiler, she managed to knock three other boilers off their stands. 'The men ran the first time after I got the three boilers, which I didn't blame them for, but after that they just used to stand there and carry on with their job,' she laughed.

Another female worker interviewed by Rosa Matheson began in 'R' Shop 'scragging' nuts — a dirty job described earlier in this book; moving on to the Fitting Shop, she did a stint on the bomb-production line before settling into a job which she loved the best, that of 'rivet-hotting'. Working with an older riveter, she would collect and sort rivets and then heat them up to red-hot in a small furnace before picking them up with a pair of metal tongs and throwing them up to the riveter when needed. 'This was a hard job, especially in the summer, 'cos it got so hot and we had to wear overalls and a heavy leather apron.' [15] At times she, like Violet Joynes, earned more than her railwayman father, although she noted that her gang worked hard; 'There was no slacking,' she remembered.

Alice Matthews, interviewed in 1995, [16] recalled being given the choice of industry or the forces in a letter from the Labour Exchange in Swindon. Choosing the former, she was told to report to the main entrance of the railway works at 8 o'clock the following morning. She ended up working in 'X' Shop, where trackwork points and crossings had been manufactured before the war. Most of the staff in the shop were what she described as 'elderly men' who did not welcome her

Railway work continued at Swindon whenever possible. Here, in the Boiler Shop, a female member of staff is engaged in drilling holes in a locomotive firebox.

with any enthusiasm! The workshop was now involved in the production of casings for 1,000lb bombs, and Alice's job was to drill and tap four small holes in the bomb, although she confessed almost 60 years later that she really had no idea of what was expected of her and had wondered: 'What on earth am I doing here?' When interviewed she still had mixed feelings about her time in the works, recalling vividly the dirt and smell of the place but also the fact that (as already noted) female staff were relatively well paid; it was in the works that she saw her first £5 note!

As Alice Matthews found out, the men who had worked at Swindon for decades did not universally welcome the coming of women to the workshops. Many workmen resented the changes and were openly hostile, but most of the women who worked there remember being treated well and with respect. Rosa Matheson writes that in many ways the women employed in the works were in an impossible position, being accused either of a lack of commitment or (if they strove to succeed) of seeking to take men's jobs permanently. Add to this the fact that some men thought that they were earning too much money for their sex, and they could not win!

In the 1946 *Railwaymen's Year Book* a valedictory article was published which typified the prevailing attitude towards women workers on the railway. Noting that during the war more than 130,000 women had been employed on Britain's railways, it highlighted the fact that they had not, as some might have imagined, tackled 'light jobs' but had been employed in almost every duty except that of engine-driver or fireman (a closed shop they never managed to infiltrate). 'Many thousands did jobs which had never previously been considered within the capabilities of the so-called "weaker sex",'[17] the article continued. Interestingly, the anonymous writer of this piece also recognised that, as well as contributing to the national war effort, women railway workers 'came home each day after a gruelling shift only to pull up arrears on the home front'. Optimistically, the article concluded that 'at one time it was considered that women workers on railways were useful only in times of labour shortage' but that the events of World War 2 had shown that women had a more permanent place in the railway world. It was obvious, the author noted; 'Many thousands not formerly engaged on railways have *come to stay.*' This was not entirely true, however; following the end of hostilities the number of women dropped rapidly, as male staff returned from the forces. The figure of just over 95,000 women employed by the four main-line railways in September 1945 had fallen to just over 58,000 a year later. As Rosa Matheson has written, whilst many women employed in the railway works at Swindon and elsewhere on the Great Western were more than happy to relinquish their positions, there were certainly many others who would rather have continued, given the choice.

Most women missed the excitement and camaraderie they experienced in the works and the relatively high wages they had been able to earn whilst there. Things would never be the same, however, and the overall percentage of women employed by the railways did not revert to anything like its prewar level; more than 13% of the workforce was recorded as female in the 1948-50 period, as opposed to 5% in 1939, although most were now employed in a clerical capacity.

World War 2 changed the lives of all who lived through it, but its impact on Great Western staff cannot be overestimated. The difficult conditions, the Blackout, shortages, bombing and long hours all took their toll but seemed to highlight the loyalty and camaraderie of Company employees before and after the war. For the women and young male staff the war was a sometimes tough introduction to railway work, whilst for older staff who had begun their career in the Company's heyday in the 1920s or 1930s it marked a dramatic watershed. The forced nationalisation of the railways — a practical necessity during the war — became a political reality in 1948, when 'God's Wonderful Railway' was absorbed into the new British Railways organisation. Truly, things would never be the same again.

A female member of staff working in 'A' Shop, acting as a 'rivet hotter' — a task enjoyed by one of the staff interviewed in this book.

7

Miscellaneous Occupations

The final chapter of this book is, by its nature, a reflection of the many and varied jobs undertaken by staff employed by the Great Western Railway; it includes the work of some in departments already described in earlier chapters as well as those who tended to be listed at the end of a staff census because they did not fit neatly into categories or departments used by the railway.

Most travellers on the Great Western Railway in its heyday would have been hard-pressed to suggest the job of a diver as

Diver Squance pictured at Plymouth Docks in 1924.
Great Western Railway Magazine

one that might have been undertaken by an employee of the railway. To those with more knowledge of the extent of the Company and its operation the job would have been entirely logical, as by the mid-1920s it owned extensive docks and harbours in South Wales and elsewhere, many acquired when the 'Big Four' railway companies were created after World War 1. Add to this facilities at Brentford, Bridgwater, Fishguard, Fowey, Kingswear, Plymouth and Weymouth, as well as many miles of canal, and one can readily appreciate that the employment of divers was necessary.

The work of one of the Great Western's most senior divers, William Squance, was described in some detail in a candid and revealing article in the *Great Western Railway Magazine* in 1924.[1] Interestingly, the article noted that, until the aforementioned acquisition of dock facilities, the Civil Engineering Department had always retained the services of at least one diver for the important role of inspecting structures in coastal areas or on rivers. The visible parts of bridges over rivers and estuaries could easily be checked by the Civil Engineers, but divers were used to examine the foundations of bridges that were below water level, ensuring that there were no signs of wear and tear, weakness or subsidence.

Working on rivers inland was not without incident, particularly during the winter. Diver Squance reported how on one occasion, when checking the foundations of a railway bridge over a fast-flowing river, he (with some difficulty) managed to get to the bridge pier in mid-stream, before discovering that a tree trunk was blocking one of the openings. As he was attempting to free the obstruction the powerful current knocked him off his feet and threatened to carry him away. The phlegmatic diver was undaunted by the experience, and visions of him being swept away were apparently more disturbing to those watching from the bridge!

For the most part, Squance spent his time within the confines of Plymouth Docks, where, it was reported, he had worked for almost 40 years. Discussing the attributes and capabilities needed by the best divers, the author of the article noted that in general the profession was 'much maligned', comparing them to anglers, 'some of whom have a reputation for veracity'. One imagines that it would be difficult for a member of the Civil Engineer's Department to doubt or contradict the findings of someone who has just emerged dripping wet from a murky dock after fumbling about in filthy water! Thus the ideal diver was seen as one who was both competent and 'thoroughly reliable'.

Another important prerequisite was that divers should be physically tough. The diving gear used during this period would today seem very primitive, with air being pumped down to the diver from an air-pump mounted in a boat. Wearing a heavy waterproof suit, boots, the traditional iron helmet and lead weights on his back and chest, the diver descended to the bottom using what was known as a 'shot line'. This had a heavy weight attached which, before the diver submerged, was dropped into the water near to where the underwater work was to be done. As the weight dropped, the diver grabbed onto the line and was naturally (if perilously) guided to the right position. Crude though this method seems, it was necessary; in most cases the water was so murky that the diver could not see where he was supposed to be! As he descended, a member of staff in the pump boat paid out the air line and a life line. While he was working on the bottom those in the boat could see little save a trail of bubbles streaming to the surface. Communication between diver and surface was by a series of jerks on the life line, although occasionally a primitive portable telephone was used. The men at the surface could not afford to lose concentration, although the author of the article reflected that, after so many years working together, the understanding between members of the team was almost telepathic.

The day-to-day work of the diver included the inspection of the foundations of docks and jetties, the repair and renewal of mooring chains and buoys and the removal of any obstructions or hazards in shipping channels. Diver Squance was also called upon to work on the dock gates at Plymouth when they were removed for repair or renewal, as well as to undertake the inspection of ships' hulls, in order to avoid prohibitively expensive dry docking. The magazine article reported that his services were also required to recover cargo dropped from vessels in deep water, most notably the risky operation of salvaging mail and passenger baggage lost when the Great Western steamship *The Ibex* sank in the English Channel in 1901.

A panoramic view of Plymouth Docks recorded just after World War 1.
Two of the Company's ships can be seen on the right. *National Railway Museum*

Above:
The scene at Cardiff Docks in 1946, with passengers embarking on RMS *St Hilary* as GWR staff load their luggage ready for the voyage.

Right:
Wagons shunted to the dockside await the cargo being unloaded from a Greek ship at Cardiff Docks in the 1930s.

Carrying out his job in conditions that were frequently less than ideal, Diver Squance was said to have had more than his fair share of 'close shaves' during his 40-year career. On one occasion, when he was working at a depth of more than 80ft, the safety line suddenly dropped another dozen or so feet. This, compounded by the increased pressure, rendered him temporarily unconscious, but, regaining his faculties, he managed to signal for his support crew to haul him to safety. The article reported that, despite passing out, after a few moments he 'returned to the bottom and completed his work'! Concluding his pen portrait of this tough and brave member of Great Western staff, the author recorded that the diver had become 'acquainted with the denizens of the deep, their haunts and habits' and that 'one could write a volume on the experiences of a railway diver'.

Divers like William Squance would have had a fair degree of contact with dock foremen, who had a responsible and busy job, particularly at a location such as Cardiff Docks, where Walter Chapple was Chief Dock Foreman in 1939. He identified as his main responsibility the loading and discharging of steamers 'of any size and type from tramp to cargo and liner to tug'. In a dock like Cardiff ships would be unloading a wide variety of cargoes — esparto grass, fruit, zinc, lead, timber, iron and cattle. Unlike today, when many cargoes are carried in large metal containers which can be easily loaded and unloaded, before World War 2 unloading cargo from ships could be slow and laborious. It was the dock foreman's task to supervise this process, ensuring that

Above left:
Staff using a conveyor to load flour into a warehouse at Cardiff Docks.

Left:
Staff busy unloading a cargo of Canadian flour at Cardiff in August 1946.

Right:
Cased oranges awaiting distribution from one of the warehouses at Cardiff in March 1951.

the cargo was placed so that the items stowed did not obstruct material required for the next port of call. It was also necessary to make sure that cargo was distributed evenly in the hold and stowed securely so that it would not move in rough seas.

In the case of ships being unloaded, the foreman was responsible for requesting the right number of railway wagons to carry the imported cargo. Most importantly, he had also to decide how many men were needed to carry out the process of loading or unloading. Men were normally organised into gangs according to the complexity of the task and whether the cargo needed to be discharged into rail wagons immediately or a warehouse within the docks itself. As at most docks, the labourers employed to unload the cargoes were usually casual. Men would turn up early each morning, looking for work, and the foreman and his staff would then engage enough to cover the day's quota. As Chapple noted, there were always more men than he required, and quite often he would be faced with 300 men chasing fewer than 150 jobs — a situation exacerbated in the 1930s during the Great Depression. The foreman's experience and his knowledge of the items to be unloaded aided the selection process.

During the 1930s large numbers of cattle were imported into the United Kingdom through ports like Cardiff. Citing the example of the unloading of the SS *Dakotian*, Chapple described how the whole process began at 5am. The men he had chosen were standing by, and, once gangways had been

secured, the signal was given for the animals to be untied and driven ashore. Separated into pens and then fed with hay, the cattle required further attention, since the cows needed to be milked before they could be moved elsewhere; if they were to be sold at the Docks, they would have to be washed down and their stalls cleaned out in readiness.

In the case of fruit, which was also imported in vast quantities at this time, the process was somewhat different. Fruit would be unloaded and stored in temperature-controlled warehouses while samples were sent to market for auction. Once the various lots were auctioned, consignment orders were then back to the Docks, and the foreman had then rapidly to organise the loading into railway wagons to ensure that the fruit arrived at its destination the next day. Indeed, Chapple concluded his description of his job by noting that, although there were many busy people at the Docks, none was busier than the Chief Dock Foreman!

Although the railways ultimately hastened the decline of the canal system they largely replaced, the Great Western and other railway companies either absorbed or maintained interests in canals which they needed for purposes of trans-shipment. One such was the Kennet & Avon Canal, which by the early years of the 20th century had largely been rendered obsolete by the London–Bristol main line. However, trade up and down the waterway was still sufficient to justify the employment of a Canal Traffic Inspector at Bradford-on-Avon. According to the *Great Western Railway Magazine* of September 1902, the then holder of this post, Inspector

The General Stores at Swindon in October 1933. The stores were situated to the east of the Gloucester branch, close to the locomotive shed. *National Railway Museum*

A. Weston, performed a very courageous act in July of that year, when he dived fully clothed into the canal to rescue a boy who had fallen in while fishing. This boy was in fact the 10th person to be saved by the inspector, who had also bravely plucked a woman from a lock in the middle of winter. A similar deed was reported in the same edition, whereby a lock-keeper employed by the GWR at London-derry Wharf, near Bath, had rescued a five-year-old girl from the water and resuscitated her in August 1902.[2]

Returning to dry land, a multitude of staff was employed in the General Stores at Swindon. Located in a large warehouse to the east of the Gloucester branch line, the Stores supplied equipment not only to the workshops but also to stations and depots all over the Great Western network. Held here were stocks of all items needed to run the railway, other than signalling equipment and clocks (dealt with separately by the Signal Works at Reading) — and, of course, locomotives and rolling stock!

The shelves of the Stores were crammed with the sort of everyday material now eagerly collected by railway enthusiasts: furniture, office equipment, hand tools, nails, screws — virtually anything required by the railway! If a stationmaster at a remote rural station in Mid Wales needed a broom to allow his lad porter to sweep the platforms, he would fill in the necessary requisition form and send or telegraph it to the Stores at Swindon, whereupon a new broom would be dispatched on a 'stores van'. Such wagons were normally attached to the rear of scheduled services and would call at stations on a regular basis, delivering stores and equipment as required. The stationmaster would, of course, be obliged to return the old worn-out broom to the stores, not only to prove that it had not been pilfered by staff but also so that the handle could be recycled, this usually being cut down and used as handles for hammers or other hand tools!

Besides those staff confined to the General Stores in Swindon were the travelling stores inspectors. One such was Charles Davis, who, like many in this book, spent his entire life working for the Great Western Railway.[3] He joined the service of the Company in 1913, beginning his career in the Stores Office at Birkenhead; after serving in the Royal Marines during World War 1 he moved to Swindon, where he stayed until his retirement.

Above: The Travelling Stores van arriving at a station in the Wolverhampton area.

Below: A cartoon, produced at Swindon Works, of Travelling Stores Inspector Charles Davis. *Deborah Guest collection*

Although based at the Stores, Charles spent every other week travelling around the network, dealing with queries about fuel, stationery, furniture, stock and supplies of all kinds. Such was the knowledge and experience gained on his travels, he claimed, that he could recite, in order, the name of every station and halt on the system; considering that there were well over 500, this was no mean feat! During the 1930s there was a popular radio series featuring a detective named Hornleigh, and this became Charles's nickname in the Stores Offices, given that his job involved a great deal of detective work, tracking and auditing stores that had gone missing, either through carelessness or as the result of theft. On one occasion during the dark days of World War 2, when the temptations of the black market frequently saw equipment and materials disappear, he was given the task of tracking down a large consignment of office equipment which had gone astray. At the end of a fruitless day of searching he was shown to his hotel room in Wolverhampton, only to find it full of the furniture he was looking for!

To facilitate his extensive travels around the Great Western network Charles was given both a free pass and a 'carriage key'

that enabled him to let himself into locked carriage compartments. On one occasion, having only just managed to catch a train at Bath, he let himself, panting, into a First-class carriage. Settling down for the journey, he looked up to find himself sitting opposite a rather elegant elderly lady; to his shock, it was none other than HM Queen Mary, who was on her way to Badminton, where she spent much of the war with her niece, the Duchess of Beaufort. A further useful aid was a pass key allowing him access to waiting rooms and other offices, and on another occasion he used this to open the locked door of the First-class waiting rooms at Paddington, only to come face-to-face with a rather menacing-looking man brandishing a revolver. Discovering that this was in fact the Emperor Haile Selassie's bodyguard, Charles made his excuses and found somewhere else to wait for his train!

During World War 2 much of Charles's time was spent on salvage work for the war effort. Given the pressures on the supply of raw materials, especially after the fall of France and the Dunkirk evacuation, keeping a close eye on all stores, especially coal and oil, was very important. The Company set up a 'Salvage Corps' and, as well as having dumps for all types of material at most stations and depots, converted a number of special salvage wagons, which toured the network collecting material for reuse. Such was the success of this campaign that at one stage over 500 tons of iron and steel was reportedly being dealt with per week.

Permanent-way staff at work on a major project re-laying track outside Paddington station in August 1924.

Like many staff, Charles met his future wife while working for the railway. Annie Matthews worked in the offices dealing with the oil accounts, adding the seemingly endless columns of figures quickly and accurately; at this time oil-lamps were still used at many locations on the railway, and every drop of oil had to be accounted for! Charles and Annie were married in 1926, after which Annie would, according to the Company's rules, have had to resign from its service.

If staff at Swindon Works regarded the job of boilermaker as one of the most unpleasant in the Factory, on the railway as a whole, it is probably true to say that, in the opinion of most railwaymen, absolutely the worst job was that of the Permanent Way staff, particularly the platelayers and gangers, who laid and repaired the track and maintained fences, drains and other lineside structures. Although most of this group were classified as 'unskilled' labour, a good platelayer needed experience and initiative, as well as strength and endurance. Nor should the importance of this job be underestimated; if work on the permanent way were not correctly carried out, the consequences could be not only expensive but also potentially disastrous.

In 1928 E. S. Hadley, the editor of the *Great Western Railway Magazine*, spent a week as a platelayer, and the article that resulted from his experiences gives a unique insight into the role. After a stringent medical to ensure that he was fit enough to carry out the job, Hadley was put to work in a gang that was responsible for maintaining part of the main line in the London area. Under the control of a ganger, a group of men looked after a stretch of line that varied in length according to the number of tracks and complexity of pointwork but might be up to a mile and a half long. On a small rural branch line, however, a gang might care for a much longer stretch of track.

The most important task for the ganger and his team was to walk his 'length' regularly, to check for any broken rails, fishplates or bolts and to ensure that any track keys that had worked loose were hammered back in. Permanent-way staff also examined the joints between rails, to see that they were set at the correct distance for expansion. As a further safety check, permanent-way inspectors, who supervised gangers and their men, were instructed to walk over the whole of their allotted district at least once a fortnight.

A surviving fragment of an inspector's report, dating from 1939, for the Risca District in South Wales gives a fascinating insight as to how methodical and safety-conscious the railway was and also how fit its staff must have been! On the first day of his duty, a Sunday, the unnamed inspector had worked re-laying the track at the up loop at Abercarn station, as well as changing a 'slack rail'. Over the following days he walked the line from Abercarn to Cwmcarn, checking the Penar Colliery branch from Markham Colliery

A classic view of a ganger walking his length of track, examining and checking as he goes.

down to Oakdale and the line from Aberbeeg to Cwm as well as various other stretches of line in the area, in so doing covering a distance of more than 10 miles.

Staff began their shift at 7am, with a half-hour break between 8.30 and 9am. When Hadley worked with the gang in London he was told to bring his own food each day, which was cooked by a member of the gang in their lineside hut. Breakfast was served after an hour and a half of work removing and oiling the fishplates that joined track together. Hadley described how the oil used was the consistency of treacle or tar. Handling the equipment, he got oil splashed all over his hands; as he wiped the perspiration from his face, the sticky mixture was transferred there too. Before sitting down to breakfast, staff wiped their hands as best they could with oily waste (in the same way as Swarfega hand-cleaner would be used today) and a piece of sacking which was used as a towel.

The editor of the staff magazine was clearly surprised by

the close friendship shared by the gang and by the wide variety of topics discussed in the meal breaks. 'Their interest in the topics of the day, their intelligent views, and the extent of their general knowledge was a revelation to me,' he noted.[4] Having to work so closely together as a team in all weathers no doubt bred a team spirit seldom seen anywhere else on the railway; one of the main reasons other staff looked down somewhat on permanent-way staff was the fact that they had to be out on duty in all weathers, summer and winter.

The weather affected permanent-way work perhaps more than that of any other department, in that it controlled when certain operations could be carried out. For example, the lifting and packing of track with ballast was usually done in the winter or early spring, but only if the ground itself were not too wet or frozen with frost. Prolonged bad weather could cause particular problems; if heavy rain persisted, then the sodden ground could eventually give way and slip, or soil could block drains causing floods. The Great Western's Divisional Engineer at Bristol urged his inspectors: 'In storms of excessive rain, snow, or in gales of wind, you must pay special attention to any part of your district most likely to be affected and where slips are liable to occur you must arrange for watchmen to be on duty night and day to protect the trains.'[5] That permanent-way staff were out in all weathers was reflected in the fact that they were issued with special clothing, although a letter from the General Manager's Office in the 1930s, written by a Mr J. F. Lean and giving details of their clothing allowance — one brown

The sheer strength needed to be a ganger is apparent from this picture, taken at Slough, of a large group lifting a sizeable piece of trackwork without the aid of a crane.

Re-laying track, this time with a steam crane, at Maidenhead in 1946. *National Railway Museum*

mackintosh every two years, one pair of leather leggings every three years, one suit of blue-jean overalls every two years — suggests that little account was taken of the likely wear and tear.[6]

In very hot weather gangers and platelayers were kept busy loosening track bolts to allow for expansion — an operation that had to be reversed in the evening when the temperature had dropped. Continuous welded rail has now rendered this whole operation unnecessary, and the regular 'clickety click' of the rail joints has ceased to be a familiar part of rail travel.

If a length of track were to be re-laid entirely, plans to carry out the work would normally be made weeks in advance, as this was usually done on a Sunday when the line was completely closed for an 'occupation'. Staff worked against the clock, removing the old, worn-out rail and replacing it with the new. The work having been completed to the satisfaction of the inspector, the relevant stretch of line was handed back to the Traffic Department, and a speed restric-tion of 15mph imposed. For the next few days the gang would spend time packing additional ballast, slewing and putting final touches to their work before it was inspected once again, this time by the Divisional Inspector, who, if happy, would pass it and remove the speed restriction.

Platelayers would also be called upon to effect running repairs on trackwork; these might involve removing a rotten or damaged sleeper or replacing a cast-iron track chair that had cracked. All this work was heavy and awkward; lifting and manœuvring sleepers and other track fittings was not for the faint-hearted, even with the help of jacks and other implements, and minor accidents must have been commonplace. An accident report from 1941 records that a ganger, one Richard Wall, who worked on the line at Buildwas in Herefordshire, was injured whilst loading track chairs into a rail wagon after an occupation. The unfortunate ganger suffered a black eye when one of his workmates, who clearly was not concentrating, struck him

The dangers of working on the track are shown in this posed safety picture showing a ganger with his foot trapped in a point!

on the right eyebrow, 'cutting it open and causing it to blacken and swell badly'.[7]

More serious was the risk of being injured by passing trains whilst working on the track. Detailed statistics are difficult to analyse, but in a lecture given to the Great Western Lecture & Debating Society in 1911, H. D. Anderson revealed that in the previous five years 174 staff had been killed and 2,502 injured in accidents to trains and the movement of railway vehicles: these included not only railway crashes proper but also fatalities and accidents to shunters and lineside staff. In the previous decade the number of staff killed each year had averaged almost 40 — not a good statistic, even though some railways, such as the London & North Western, were significantly worse. It was not surprising, therefore, to discover that the railway spent a good deal of time warning staff about the dangers they faced, identifying that many accidents were due to human error. In his lecture Anderson stressed that he did not want to give the impression

'that railwaymen are as a class either unintelligent, reckless or indifferent; on the contrary they are, taken all round, as fine a body of men as any in the kingdom'.[8]

The perils facing track staff were made plain in the Great Western's 'Safety Movement' booklet, published in 1914. A whole chapter was devoted to the dangers of crossing the railway, and various examples were cited of accidents in which staff had been killed or injured. One such was that of a member of the Engineering Department who, while walking on the sleepers of a loop at Bradford-on-Avon, was knocked down by a train. As the author noted, 'When you're lying injured on the ground it's too late to ask yourself IS IT SAFE?'[9]

In the final chapter of the booklet the Company detailed all personal accidents on the GWR, department by department, for the month of October 1913. Within the Engineering Department (which employed permanent-way staff), a total of 183 staff had been injured, with two killed.

Amongst this total 22 had been injured unloading sleepers, a further 17 unloading and stacking rail and six through tripping or stumbling on the line. A further 103 minor accidents, classed by the Company as 'miscellaneous' — cuts, sprains and strains — were also recorded. Little wonder, then, that the 1914 'Safety Movement' booklet was reissued after World War 1 and that Health & Safety (as we now know it) remained a major issue throughout the Company's existence and beyond.

Working on the line every day no doubt led to a certain degree of carelessness and complacency, and, as a result, staff needed to be kept alert at all times. One of the key men on the team, therefore, was the 'look-out', whose job it was to keep a watchful eye open for approaching trains and to blow either a whistle or horn to warn staff of their imminent arrival. The Company rulebook was very clear about procedures in this case. As well as his whistle or horn, the look-out — who had to be deemed 'competent' by the permanent-way inspector — was to be equipped with at least a dozen detonators (small charges that were laid on the rails and exploded as a warning when a train passed over them) and with red and green flags, as well as a hand lamp in snow, fog or poor light. Particular care was needed at locations where visibility was a problem, namely reverse curves and tunnels, where look-outs were positioned further away to ensure that staff working on the line had ample time to retreat to a safe position when a train approached.

As well as being involved in the heavy work associated with the upkeep of the permanent way, staff were expected to maintain the land around the railway itself. This involved ensuring that fencing was in good order; livestock escaping onto the line could not only cause a hazard to trains but might also leave the Company open to insurance claims if it were proved that its fences or walls had allowed valuable animals to stray. Gangers and platelayers kept lineside vegetation down, clearing undergrowth and trees, and in some cases grass cut from embankments could be sold as hay; the instructions issued to inspectors in 1903 by the Divisional Engineer in Bristol stated that they should 'always endeavour to obtain the best offers for grass on the slopes and submit the same to me for approval'.

In long, hot summers permanent-way staff had to be on their guard against lineside fires which might be caused by stray sparks from the steam locomotives passing along their length of line. A circular issued in May 1939 jointly by the Superintendent of the Line, the Chief Mechanical Engineer and the Chief Engineer reminded staff of the danger. 'During the summer months and especially in dry periods special look-out is required, and immediate steps must be taken by all concerned to extinguish fires and so avoid serious consequences.'[10]

Concluding his affectionate portrait of the staff with whom he had worked during his stint as a platelayer, E. S. Hadley noted that 'because of his hobnail boots and dust-laden and oil-soaked clothes [the platelayer] received sparse consideration and scant respect'.[11] Clearly, judging by the work described here, one is inclined to agree; as a group, permanent-way staff have probably never been accorded the respect they truly deserve amongst railway workers. Without their hard and sometimes dangerous work in all weathers, the crack expresses and humble goods trains run by the Company could not have made their way safely around the Great Western network.

One of the more recognisable railway jobs to most travellers in the steam era was that of the 'wheel-tapper', known more correctly as a carriage- or wagon-examiner. There was, of course, rather more to the job than merely tapping wheels with a hammer. Writing in 1937, carriage-examiner J. A. Taylor of Birkenhead noted that songs had been written about his job and that the travelling public were not above making jokes about the 'Knight of the Hammer', as he was known. The rather less glamorous task undertaken by the carriage-examiner was to ensure that every vehicle used on passenger services was 'fit for the road' and moreover that, once it was shunted into a train, it remained in good condition. By the 1930s rolling stock was being used far more intensively than in earlier times (albeit nowhere near as intensively as is the case today!), and use in trains with average speeds of over 80mph meant that it needed close attention.

Many a carriage-examiner began his career at 16 as a greaser and oiler — another filthy job that involved the oiling of axles, draw gear, buffers, brakes and other fittings. Crawling around and under carriage stock in all weathers was good training, giving staff a sound basic knowledge of the workings and layout of Great Western carriages. After a few years the next step was to progress to the repair depot, after which there would be a stint within the Carriage & Wagon Department at Swindon, where training in the duties of an examiner followed. Having duly passed an examination by one of the senior inspectors, staff would be posted to locations all over the Great Western network.

Responsible for the whole train except the locomotive itself, the carriage-examiner needed a working knowledge of almost all aspects of train operation, including the vacuum-braking system, the lighting (whether it be electric or gas-powered) and the steam-heating system. His area of responsibility extended to within the carriages themselves, such that he addressed complaints regarding stiff door handles and missing window straps. If a member of the public complained about the rough riding of a carriage, the initial investigation would be carried out by the

A picture illustrating just how much work there would have been for a wagon inspector or examiner in South Wales in the 1930s. The scene acts as a telling reminder of how much has changed with the demise of the area's coal industry. *National Railway Museum*

An inspector at work, sitting on the side of a coal wagon, somewhere in South Wales in the 1920s.

examiner; if he could find no fault with the vehicle, the Engineering Department would become involved, using what became known as the 'whitewash coach', fitted with special equipment which, on hitting a rough section, dumped white paint on the track, allowing it to be identified by permanent-way staff!

At the end of his article J. A. Taylor returned to the theme of wheel-tapping. During his 28-year career as a carriage-examiner, he declared, he had identified many worn wheels or flanges, but, thanks to the process of regular examination, he had come across only one cracked tyre.[12]

A few months after Taylor's recollections had been published in the staff magazine it was the turn of his colleagues in the Goods Department to have their place in the spotlight. The wagon-examiner shared the same tool of choice — the wheel-tapper's hammer — but there, according to E. H. Ingledon, from Cardiff Docks, the similarities ended. The job of the wagon-examiner, he argued, was to look at coal wagons before and after they were tipped and at

goods wagons and vans before they were loaded up. In the case of coal wagons, at Cardiff Docks they arrived from collieries further up the South Wales Valleys and were then shunted into sidings before being 'tipped', the coal ending up in the hold of colliers bound for destinations all over the world. The whole process of tipping and the treatment the wagons received at the collieries made them far more prone to damage, so a close watch was required to ensure that brake gear, couplings and buffers, as well as the woodwork and strapping, were in good shape. 'Wagons are more likely to be defective because they do not get such gentle handling as their more handsome relations,' wrote Ingledon.[13]

Inspections of wagons withdrawn from service as defective and visits to wagon-repair shops were all part of the job; once repairs were complete wagons could be passed as safe to be used. An example of the work done by the examiner is provided by a report made in May 1925 at Westbury yard, where an ex-Lancashire & Yorkshire Railway open goods wagon had been discovered some days before, its floor

A more recent photograph of a wagon inspector, taken in 1973. The subject of the picture is Walter Hayward, who was based at Swindon.

saturated with acid. The report noted that the wagon had been loaded with two bottles of acid, one at each end, inside a half a barrel. Sent from the General Stores at Swindon to the locomotive sheds at Westbury and Salisbury, they had obviously been in a 'rough shunt', causing them to break. The report recommended that the wagon be sent back to Swindon, where the Carriage & Wagon Department would have to sort out the mess![14]

As well as looking at 'cripples' the wagon-examiner checked that wagons used for special loads — many of which carried exotic names, such as 'Macaws' or 'Crocodiles', given to them for identification purposes — were safe to carry these to their destinations. Compared with that of the carriage-examiner, the job of the wagon-examiner was much less salubrious. Tramping around the 'muddy dock sides and dust-laden empty tip roads' was surely not the highlight of any railway career but was nevertheless a vital task, as the express train and the goods had to run with equal safety on the road.

Although Swindon Works had a large Carpenter's Shop within the Carriage & Wagon Works, where much of the equipment seen on stations (such as sack trucks and parcels trolleys) was manufactured and repaired, there were a number of other carpenters' workshops based at depots elsewhere on the GWR network. These depots, run by the Engineering Department, were responsible for the maintenance not only of equipment but also of property in the areas they served.

In 1990 Tom Fish wrote a fascinating account of his experiences as an apprentice carpenter at the Great Western depot at West Ealing.[15] This was huge, comprising various separate sections that included Blacksmiths, Bricklayers & Masons, Painting & Glazing, Carpenters & Wood Mill and Plumbing & Tinsmiths. The Advertising & Publicity section also had a presence in the yard, being responsible for special work such as decorating Paddington station for Royal arrivals/departures or Henley station for the Regatta. The depot served more than 30 stations, both on the main line between Paddington and Slough/Windsor and on all the local branch lines in between, the locomotive depots at Old Oak Common, Southall and Slough and the docks at Brentford, as well as the stations on the old Great Western/Great Central joint line as far as High Wycombe.

Tom began his apprenticeship in the last years of the Great Western Railway proper, starting work in the summer of 1946. Once again, family ties were to the fore, as his father was also a carpenter employed by the Company at Paddington. During his three-month probationary period Tom worked with no pay, beginning with very mundane tasks such as sandpapering the hundreds of feet of wooden mouldings that were used on station nameboards. Miles of this timber was needed, because during World War 2, which

No picture survives of the Carpenter's Shop at West Ealing. This was its counterpart at Swindon in 1953.

had only recently ended, all such nameboards had been taken down, and many now needed repair or replacement. Many were new, but the cast-iron letters from the old boards had been retained and were screwed back onto the new backing boards when required.

In true Great Western fashion, Tom was eventually teamed up with an older carpenter, Frank Hemmings, who taught him his trade. Tom remembered that the carpenters' shop in which he worked was largely involved in building maintenance, like producing new doors for engine sheds where locomotive drivers had failed to stop in time. These doors were not small, being up to 16ft high, 10ft wide and around 4in thick. He also recalled building level-crossing gates, of which one pair were 16ft across, requiring the Blacksmith's Shop to make metal harnesses and straps to support their weight. Other odd jobs tackled by the carpenters included the manufacture of picture frames for the offices at Paddington, wooden toolboxes and carrying-cases; they even designed and produced a wooden depth-

gauge, used by the boatmen at Brentford Docks to measure the depth of water in the basin. Other staff carried out more specific tasks, one spending almost all his time repairing the hundreds of barrows and parcels trucks used at Paddington, while another had the responsibility of repairing many of the canvas blinds used both in ticket offices at stations and in the vast office complex at Paddington.

Many of the men employed by the Engineering Department used the West Ealing depot as a base but spent much time away working at various locations in the area. Most would 'clock in' using a special time clock on the station platform and return only to collect their wages from the depot. Off-site work done by carpenters included the repair of fixtures and fittings at stations and railway booking offices (such as waiting-room and toilet doors) and the replacement of decking and stair treads on footbridges. The least popular jobs involved repairs to engine sheds, particularly the roofs. Worst of all was replacing the smoke vents; this required the dismantling of the old structure,

A railway carpenter on the job at Swindon, as featured in the *Western Region Magazine* in 1958.

joined at a very important and momentous time; George Jackson Churchward, the Company's charismatic Chief Mechanical Engineer, had retired the previous year, and his successor, C. B. Collett, was busy designing what became some of the most famous Great Western locomotives in its history. The 'Castle' class of express passenger engines was already in production, and within a few years Low's section was to produce further famous designs like the 'King', 'Hall' and 'Manor' classes. Most of his work as a junior draughtsman, however, was concerned with the modification of locomotives acquired from the many constituent and subsidiary railways taken over by the Great Western in 1923. The so-called 'Great Westernising' of these engines, from such as the Taff Vale Railway and the Cardiff Railway, required Low and his colleagues to study old tracings and drawings and, frequently, to make detailed sketches of locomotives for which no drawings were available; the designs were then altered to incorporate the maximum number of standard Great Western parts.

After a further year Low found himself in a team investigating the feasibility of electrifying the main line west of Taunton, this involving much work away from the Factory, producing timings and details of locomotive performance. Although he and a number of other staff did considerable work on this project, ultimately it came to nothing, and he returned to the Locomotive Drawing Office proper. There was, however, a short interlude in 1926 during the General Strike, when he and 14 other draughtsmen volunteered for work on the footplate. Employed thus in the Chippenham area, Low nevertheless noted later, with some sadness: 'I might mention that the atmosphere at home was somewhat strained, as both my father and brother were on strike.' This was probably something of an understatement, hiding what would likely have been a very difficult situation. The majority of the workforce at Swindon was solidly behind the strike, and when the men went back to work there was some tension between the strikers and the so-called 'blacklegs' — a scenario repeated all over the network.

By the early 1930s Low had gained sufficient experience to be admitted to the salaried staff as a 'senior clerk'. At the time

invariably covered in years of soot and grime which would fall on everything, including the Engineering Department staff. Extra 'dirt' money was paid, but this scarcely compensated them for the discomfort!

The final occupation to be described in this survey of miscellaneous jobs involves a return to the great works at Swindon, where there has been extensive coverage of what happened on the shop floor but less of an emphasis on the clerical side. The following is based on an account of his career written by R. J. Low in 1963 entitled 'Forty Years in the Locomotive Drawing Office'.[16] This was eventually published in the British Railways Western Region magazine, but some of the more irreverent asides in the original were edited out, most notably the subtitle describing his career in the works as a 'life sentence'!

Low entered the Drawing Office in 1923 and was immediately posted to the locomotive section. He had this would normally have required him to sit a 'clerk's examination', but fortunately he was 'excused this indignity' on account of having a Matriculation Certificate from school. He nevertheless had to go to Paddington to be interviewed by the Appointments Board, which meant an overnight stay at the Company's expense. The end result was a rise of £9 per annum, bringing his salary to £230 a year before stoppages such as tax and pension contribution. A few years later, during the Depression, salaries would be cut by up to 3%.

Further design work followed on locomotives such as the '2251' 0-6-0 tender engines and various tank-engine classes. Low recalled that during World War 2 18 draughtsmen from all parts of the office were allowed to join up; for the rest of the team war work dominated, as little new production could be attempted. Interestingly, although the Drawing Office dealt with various projects, Low felt that 'the technical potential of the offices was not used to the full and many of us had a feeling of frustration'.

After the war Low worked on a variety of projects, including the conversion of some locomotives to burn oil and, later, those British Railways standard designs built at Swindon. When he finally retired in 1963 he had served under five Chief Mechanical Engineers of the Great Western and British Railways (Western Region) and eight Chief Draughtsmen. Having worked in the same Drawing Office for 40 years, he estimated that he had climbed the stairs to the office at least 40,000 times! He was leaving the railway at a time of great change, and had already worked through years of tremendous upheaval. The decline of the steam locomotive and the rise of the diesel were followed by a decline in the stature and importance of the great railway works at Swindon. If the changes there were a metaphor for the changes elsewhere on the railway at the time, then Low was clearly pessimistic: the railway he had grown up with was changing rapidly — and not for the best, he felt. He had, he wrote, been in a 'happy office' where he had 'come to terms with life' but was not so hopeful about the future of the Drawing Office 'in this brave new world of re-shapings and redundancies'. For Low and many other staff, the railway world they knew and in which they had grown up was about to change dramatically and, for most, not for the better. That world would, within 10 years, be completely transformed, and a modern era of railway working would consign many of the traditions and working practices described here to the history books and to the memories of those who worked on God's Wonderful Railway.

One side of the Drawing Office at Swindon Works, where R. J. Low worked and where many of the most famous GWR classes were designed.

References & Bibliography

General

Adams, W. (Ed): *Encyclopædia of the Great Western Railway*, PSL Books, 1990

Joby, R. S.: *The Railwaymen*, David & Charles, 1984

McKenna, F.: *The Railway Workers 1840-1970*, Faber, 1980

Russell, J. K.: *Great Western Company Servants*, Wild Swan Publications, 1983

Simmons, J. and Biddle, G. (Eds): *The Oxford Companion to Railway History*, Oxford University Press, 1997

Introduction

1 Dawson, W.: 'Selecting, Training and Disciplining Railway Staff', GWR Lecture & Debating Society Proceedings, 31 March 1905
2 GWR form, May 1919 (STEAM Collection)
3 *Great Western Progress*, Great Western Railway, 1935 (p113)
4 Pole, F.: 'The Element of Chance in a Railway Career — Could it be Minimised?', GWR Lecture & Debating Society Proceedings, 2 December 1909
5 GWR report (STEAM Collection)
6 *GWR Magazine*, July 1940 (p79)

Chapter 1

1 Hyde, D. J., and Atkins, A.: *GWR Goods Services*, Wild Swan Publications, 2000 (p3)
2 Ibid (p13)
3 'GWR Goods Rates and Station Working', GWR, Paddington, 1920 (p62)
4 GWR 'Fortnightly Return of Goods Stolen, Lost or Pilfered', 1 April 1933 and 18 March 1938 (STEAM Collection)
5 *GWR Magazine*, November 1916 (p11)
6 'Spotlight on my Job: The Goods Checker', *GWR Magazine*, May 1937 (p296)
7 'British Railways Freight Train Facilities (Western Region)', January 1953
8 GWR Accident Statement Report, 13 April 1941 (STEAM Collection)
9 Ibid, 28 August 1944 (STEAM Collection)
10 GWR letter, Chief Goods Manager's Office, Paddington, 28 January 1942 (STEAM Collection)
11 Railway Executive Committee Handbill: 'White Labels for Goods', September 1939
12 'GWR Cartage Instruction Book', GWR, Paddington, 1939 (p63)
13 For further detail see Russell, J. K.: *GW Horse Power*, OPC, 1995

14 GWR letter (STEAM Collection)
15 GWR Lecture & Debating Society, 1908
16 'Spotlight on my Job: The Goods Guard', *GWR Magazine*, October 1937 (p481)
17 'Spotlight on my Job: Country Goods Guard', *GWR Magazine*, August 1938 (p341)
18 GWR correspondence (STEAM Collection)
19 GWR 'General Appendix to the Rules', 1936 edition (p249)
20 GWR correspondence (STEAM Collection)

This chapter also includes information from taped and informal interviews with Stan Vickery, Colin Willott and Sid Keates (courtesy STEAM — Museum of the Great Western Railway).

Chapter 2

1 All statistics taken from 'Traffic Dealt With at Stations & Goods Depots', GWR, 1933
2 James, S. T.: *The Railwaymen*, Nelson, undated (p109)
3 Carter, H. W.: 'Spotlight on my Job: The Stationmaster', *GWR Magazine*, January 1939 (p41)
4 Hadley, E. S.: 'The Ideal Stationmaster', *GWR Magazine*, March 1905 (p126)
5 Ibid
6 Extract from the *Daily Chronicle*, 10 May 1911
7 James, Ibid
8 Handwritten letter, 13 April 1951, courtesy Ian and Jane Hill, Swindon
9 GWR Circular No 1897 'Examination & Collection of Tickets', April 1938
10 Mitchell, G.: 'Spotlight on my Job: The Ticket Collector', *GWR Magazine*, September 1938 (p383)
11 Vaughan, A.: *A Pictorial Record of Great Western Signalling*, OPC, 1973
12 Copy of GWR letter, 30 October 1915, courtesy Mrs F. Cotterill, Warminster
13 Wixey, K.: 'Cheltenham & Gloucester Signalman', *Railway World*, April 1978 (pp187-9)
14 Vaughan, A.: *Exeter West Box*, Exeter West Group, 1984 (p6)
15 BR (WR) 'Notice to Employees: Misuse of Detonators', 9 October 1951
16 Vaughan, A.: *Glory Days: Western Signalman*, Ian Allan Publishing, 2000 (p24)

17 Jones, E. O.: 'Spotlight on my Job: Signalman (Double Line)', *GWR Magazine*, April 1938 (p166)
18 *Swindon Evening Advertiser*, 28 March 1957
19 *Swindon Evening Advertiser*, 18 October 1995

Other sources consulted:
Canning, D. E.: *Signalboxes, People and Trains on the Berks & Hants Line*, Ravenswing Publishing, 2000

This chapter also includes information supplied from interview given by Sid Keates.

Chapter 3

1 Gasson, H.: *Firing Days: Reminiscences of a Great Western Fireman*, OPC, 1973 (p12)
2 Barfield, A.: *When there was Steam*, Bradford Barton, 1976 (p23)
3 Summers, A. W.: *Engines Good and Bad*, OPC, 1977
4 Morgan, B., and Meyrick, B.: *Behind the Steam*, Hutchinson Books, 1973 (p20)
5 Bryan, T. F.: *The Great Western at War 1939-1945*, PSL Books, 1995 (p129)
6 'Instructions as to moving Engines in Steam', Chief Mechanical Engineer's Department Circular No 999
7 Ibid
8 Morgan, W., and Meyrick, B.: *Behind the Steam*, Hutchinson Books, 1973 (p46)
9 Quoted in McKenna, F.: *The Railway Workers 1840-1970*, Faber, 1980
10 Tony Coles collection (STEAM archive), courtesy Mrs V. Coles
11 Brown, G.: *Riding the Midnight Hour — Drama, Excitement and Fun on the Footplate 1914-1954*, published privately by the author, 1997
12 Barlow, B.: *Didcot Engineman*, Wild Swan Publications, 1994

This chapter also includes information from taped and informal conversations with Ted Abear, Tom Conduit and Gordon Shurmer.

Chapter 4

1 Copsey, J., and Clifton, M.: 'Banbury — the Shed, the Engines and the Men', *Great Western Journal* No 3, Summer 1992
2 Summers, A.: *Engines Good and Bad*, OPC, 1977 (p17)
3 'Fuel Efficiency on the Footplate', Great Western Railway, 1945 (p10)

4 Terry, E. H.: *Great Western Reflections*, OPC, 1984 (p15)
5 Hunt, A. F.: 'Descriptive Diagrams of the Locomotive', Oswestry MIC, undated
6 Kimber, M. J.: 'Questions and Answers on the Walschaerts Valve Gear as used on British Railways Standard Locomotives', published by the author, 1957
7 Abear, E.: *Through the Links at Southall and Old Oak Common*, Xpress Publishing 2000
8 GWR Circular No 6726 'Notice to Engine Drivers and Firemen: Knowledge of Roads', May 1947
9 Ibid
10 Barlow, B.: *Didcot Engineman*, Wild Swan Publications, 1994 (p202)
11 GWR Correspondence File A84547 (STEAM archive collection)
12 Lea, J.: *The GWR MAS 1865-1965*, Swindon, 1965
13 Summers, A.W.: *Engines Good and Bad*, OPC, 1977 (p17)
14 Barlow, B.: *Didcot Engineman*, Wild Swan Publications, 1994 (p219)
15 Parsons, D.: 'Spotlight on my Job, No 3: Engine Driver', *GWR Magazine*, July 1937 (p343)
16 British Railways (Western Region) Circular No 6 February 1950: 'Notice to Drivers and Firemen: Public Health (Smoke Abatement) Act 1926'
17 Ibid
18 Abear, E., Ibid (p6)
19 Street, J. W.: *I Drove the Cheltenham Flyer*, Nicholas & Watson, 1951 (p146)
20 Gasson, H.: *Footplate Days: More Reminiscences of a Great Western Fireman*, OPC, 1976 (p87)
21 Ibid, Street, J. W. (p145)

Other sources:
Austin, S.: *From the Footplate: 'Cornish Riviera Express'*, Ian Allan Publishing, 1997
Spooner, A.: *Old Oak Enginemen*, Ian Allan Publishing, 1986

Also interviews and informal conversations with Tom Conduit and Gordon Shurmer.

Chapter 5
1 Freebury, H.: *Great Western Apprentice*, Wiltshire Library and Museum Service, 1985 (p13)
2 Ibid (p14)
3 GWR circulars issued 1915-24 (STEAM Collection)

4 *GWR Magazine*, December 1915 (p319)
5 Hayward, J.: 'Hell's Kitchen' — typewritten reminiscences (STEAM Collection)
6 GWR circulars issued 1915-24 (STEAM Collection)
7 Quoted in the *Swindon Evening Advertiser*, 10 October 1985
8 Williams, A.: *Life in a Railway Factory*, Duckworth, 1915 (p82)
9 Gibbs, K.: *Great Western Apprentice in Steam*, OPC, 1988

This chapter also includes information supplied from taped interviews and informal conversations with John Fleetwood, Jack Hayward, Tony Millard and Arthur Webb, as well as many other ex-Swindon railway staff including Alf Neate, Alan Phillpot and the late Alan Peck.

Chapter 6
1 Ross, E.: *Tales of the Rails*, Bristol Broadsides Books, 1984 (p25)
2 Ibid (p25)
3 Bryan, T.: *The Great Western at War 1939-1945*, PSL Books, 1995 (pp43-50)
4 Ross, E.: Ibid (p28)
5 Morgan, W., and Meyrick, B.: *Behind the Steam*, Hutchinson Books, 1973 (p194)
6 GWR Circular No 5956: 'Air Raid Warning Arrangements', October 1939
7 Ibid
8 GWR Circular No 6132, CME Swindon, 2 May 1941
9 Ross, E.: Ibid (p37)
10 Engineman's Report, 14 May 1942 — handwritten manuscript (STEAM Collection)
11 'Accident at Cullompton' — handwritten manuscript (STEAM Collection)
12 Lee, V. P.: 'When Smoke Gets In My Eyes' — notes given to author at the GWR Museum, Swindon, 30 August 1990 (STEAM Collection)
13 Matheson, R.: 'Women and the Great Western Railway with Special Reference to Swindon Works' — D.Phil thesis, University of the West of England, October 2002 (p254)
14 Ibid (p253)
15 Ibid (p263)
16 'Skirts in the Rail Works', *Swindon Evening Advertiser*, 23 October 1995 (p17)
17 'Railway Women', *The Railwaymen's Year Book 1946* (pp81-3)

This chapter was also compiled using taped interviews and informal conversations with John Fleetwood, Violet Joynes, Gordon Shurmer, Phyllis Saunders and Arthur Webb

Chapter 7
1 Butland, W. E.: 'The Work of a Railway Diver', *GWR Magazine*, January 1924 (pp48-50)
2 Both incidents reported in *GWR Magazine*, September 1902
3 Notes on Charles Davis kindly supplied by Deborah Guest
4 Hadley, E. S.: 'The Editor as Platelayer', *GWR Magazine*, March 1928 (pp235-8)
5 'Instructions as to Duties', GWR Divisional Engineer's Office, Bristol, 6 June 1903 (STEAM Collection)
6 Letter from GWR General Manager's Office dated 8 October 1931 (STEAM Collection)
7 GWR Accident Report, 24 August 1941 (STEAM Collection)
8 Anderson, H. D.: 'Railway Accidents — Some Facts and Figures', GWR Lecture & Debating Society Proceedings, 19 December 1912
9 'The Safety Movement', Great Western Railway, 1914 (p10)
10 GWR Circular No 5119: 'Fires Alongside the Railway', May 1939
11 Ibid
12 Taylor, J. A.: 'Spotlight on my Job, No 8: Carriage Examiner', *GWR Magazine*, December 1937 (p573)
13 Ingledon, E. H.: 'Spotlight on my Job, No 14: Wagon Examiner', *GWR Magazine*, July 1938 (p297)
14 GWR form (STEAM Collection)
15 Fish, Tom G.: 'Memories of a Carpenter's Apprentice' — typewritten notes, April 1990 (STEAM Collection)
16 Low, R. J.: 'Forty Years in the Locomotive Drawing Office' — typewritten notes, July 1963 (STEAM Collection)

Index

Ticket collector at work. The main footbridge at Paddington station taken during World War 2.